Roadless Area

PAUL BROOKS

❦ ❦ ❦

Roadless Area

DRAWINGS BY THE AUTHOR

NEW YORK: *Alfred · A · Knopf*

1971

ACKNOWLEDGMENT is made for quotations from:
"In Praise of Diversity" from *Love Letters of Phyllis McGinley*, published by The Viking Press.
"Two Look at Two" from *Complete Poems of Robert Frost*. Copyright 1923 by Holt, Rinehart and Winston, Inc. Renewed 1951 by Robert Frost. Reprinted by permission of Holt, Rinehart and Winston, Inc.
"In Praise of Johnny Appleseed" from *Selected Poems* by Vachel Lindsay. Copyright 1923 by The Macmillan Company. Renewed 1951 by Elizabeth C. Lindsay. Reprinted by permission of The Macmillan Company.

L. C. catalog card number: 64–17709

THIS IS A BORZOI BOOK,
PUBLISHED BY ALFRED A. KNOPF, INC.

PUBLISHED SEPTEMBER 21, 1964
REPRINTED TWO TIMES
FOURTH PRINTING, OCTOBER 1971

Chapter 14, first published in the *World Book Year Book* under the title "The Last Stronghold of the Great Beasts," is reprinted with the permission of the editors of the *World Book Year Book*. Copyright © 1964 by Field Enterprises Educational Corporation. The other chapters have appeared in slightly different versions in *The Atlantic Monthly*, *Harper's Magazine*, *Massachusetts Audubon*, and *Horizon*.

FOR *Susie*

Foreword

THE authorship of this book, in the root sense of that word, is as much my wife's as my own; she has done more than her share of everything except the writing. If I do not refer to her on every page it is only because her presence can invariably be read between the lines. Most of the expeditions described here have been undertaken *à deux*, without professional assistance. Indeed one reason for writing about them at all is that they can be enjoyed actually as well as vicariously by almost anyone who happens to like this sort of thing. Contrary to the assumptions of many of our friends, neither special knowledge nor unnatural passion for discomfort is required. There is only one criterion. As a woman wrote to me after reading a chapter that follows: "Your wife must be quite a lady!"

"Roadless Area" is an official designation for certain tracts of land, such as the border-lakes canoe country, which are accessible solely by canoe or trail. I have used it here in a broad sense to cover not only virgin wilderness but also country where the roads, while not far distant, are irrelevant. By extension it might also apply to certain areas of thought about men's relation to wild nature. For appreciation of wild nature can be a creative act, like appreciation of painting or literature or music. As in the case of a great work of art, it has an impact on many levels. The impact deepens with closer acquaintance; familiarity with wilderness breeds not contempt but humility.

Man's craving for wilderness increases in direct proportion to growing urbanization. The more city pavements, the more suburban sidewalks, the more precious become the surviving forest trails. The countryside near our towns and cities is slowly dying of creeping conformity. Our national symbol, the bulldozer, flattens the hills, fills the ponds, and smooths our path to man-made monotony. As Phyllis McGinley says in her poem "In Praise of Diversity," we are "altering to a common way / The planet's holy heterodoxy."

Even beyond the cities, beyond the identical main streets of our towns, identical ribbons of concrete threaten the remotest wild areas with the twin blights of sameness and tameness. Wilderness on the other hand represents the very essence of diversity. Yet year by year we whittle away this priceless heritage, forgetting that it is possible for an environment, as well as for a species of animal, to become extinct. This slow process of attrition is difficult to dramatize and to publicize. A man will drain a swamp who would not go gunning for the last ivory-billed woodpecker; he will allow the grasslands to vanish bit by bit though he wouldn't shoot a whooping crane.

Of course the greatest dangers to wilderness have always come under the head of "progress": highways for faster travel, dams for water power and irrigation, drainage of marshes that reduce the ducks we want and increase the surplus crops we don't. Now atomic energy has given us power literally to move mountains and change the face of the earth. Our subjugation of the natural world around us is reaching the point where the measure of our maturity is our willingness *not* to control every inch of our environment.

This book is selective rather than comprehensive. Brief holidays have not afforded time to camp in all the national parks nor to explore more than a few of our wilderness areas. Here at most is a fair sampling. Each park we have visited has had something special to offer. The border-lakes country and Algonquin Park in Ontario provide some of the best canoeing on the continent. Olympic Park in Washington contains a unique Temperate Zone rain forest, as well as the longest wilderness beach strip on the Pacific coast. The Great Smoky Mountains Park preserves a few splendid remnants of the virgin hardwood forest that once clothed the southern Appalachians, while the open tundra of Mount McKinley Park in Alaska is the best place to see at close range America's native mammals, from grizzly bear to Dall sheep. At the opposite pole, St. John in the Virgin Islands is *sui generis:* a snakeless Eden whose wild gardens lie both above and below the sea. The other island park, Isle Royale, is again unique: an isolated community where the balance of nature is left undisturbed, where the wolves are allowed to keep the moose in check—an important laboratory in the modern science of ecology. Canyonlands in Utah—destined, I hope, for inclusion in the park system —shows how spectacularly the forces of erosion can mold a landscape over eons of time.

My wife and I have also explored roadless areas of various sorts outside the parks and forests: the canals of England (where our canoe became not so much a means of escape to the wild as a passport to the hearts of the people), Sanibel Island off the Florida coast, Mexico's Baja California. And eventually we realized the dream of every conservationist—a safari to the wilder parts of East Africa.

In the last chapter I have considered briefly a subject that deserves a volume in itself: the changing attitude of man toward wild nature throughout history. At one time such an investigation would have been principally of literary or philosophic interest. Not so today. Our remaining wilderness will survive only if we are aware of its value in terms of human culture—if we realize that it is not an anachronism in an age of science but that, on the contrary, science has given a new significance to our relationship with wild nature.

Acknowledgments

MOST of the chapters in this book have been published as articles in *The Atlantic Monthly;* the rest have appeared in *Harper's Magazine, Horizon, Massachusetts Audubon,* and the *World Book Year Book.* To the editors of these publications, and particularly to Edward Weeks of *The Atlantic,* I gratefully acknowledge permission to republish here.

I should also like to thank the many members of the National Park Service whose knowledge and whose friendship have added immeasurably to our pleasure in visiting the parks.

P.B.

Contents

Contents

Roadless Area

CHAPTER I

A Canoe on the Border Lakes

To MY wife and to me, "roadless area" is the most poetic phrase on our road map of North America. It is printed, indefinite but irresistible, across the northern edge of Minnesota, and over the border into Canada, about fifty miles west of Lake Superior. Lacking the usual spider web of red highways and black secondary roads, innocent of a single town name, the area would look barren but for the tangled blue mass of lakes.

More detailed maps show this to be the heart of the Superior National Forest of Minnesota and Quetico Provincial Park of Ontario, a combined tract of wilderness almost five million acres in extent. A century and a half ago, the great explorer Alexander Mackenzie said that there was not "a finer country in the world for the residence of uncivilized man." If he could see it today, I doubt that he would revise his judgment, though he might be appalled at the number who need uncivilizing.

Here are the oldest rocks on the surface of the earth, known as the Canadian shield; the geographical ridgepole of the continent, whence waters flow to the Atlantic, the Arctic, and the Gulf of Mexico; the historic canoe route of the Indians and fur traders and the legendary northwest passage. Here are refuges for wildlife where guns are forbidden, and for human life where cars cannot penetrate and planes may not fly.

We had already arranged for supplies and canoe, when my wife read an account of travel in this country by the Director of the Wilderness Society. He made it sound tough: long stretches of paddling, punctuated by slithering in mud, slipping in sphagnum moss, and (this from a world authority on trail work) some trouble in finding his way. "Obviously a character-forming experience," she said, "but I'm not sure that I like to have my character formed in the summertime."

The canoe, however, was waiting at Ely, Minnesota, the jumping-off place, road's end. So there we went. The town's principal business seemed to be equipping campers for life in the wilderness at its doorstep. Enter, that early August afternoon, the headquarters of one of the leading "outfitters." A barnlike room, tier on tier of canoes on racks, in the center a table on which were already laid out the supplies for our twelve-day trip and the three huge packs that would contain them. On the floor we piled the essential gear: tent, sleeping bags, air mattresses, axe, fishing tackle, binoculars. Over all soon floated a heavenly aroma as I decanted into an aluminum flask some 151 proof Hudson's Bay rum, that most effective of liquors in terms of weight, and perfect mixer with anything that will float a canoe.

Within an hour we were whisked off on the first leg of our journey. Something about our equipment—perhaps the featherweight tent from London, or my wife's insistence on traveling light (comparative term!) and leaving behind most of the potatoes—had given the wholly erroneous impression that we knew our way around in lake-country travel. Actually most of our limited canoeing experience had been on rivers, which have the virtue of always taking you the way you are going. (Even when you smash up in the rapids, the wreckage—and probably you—will continue in the right direction.) Threading your way among lakes and currentless beaver-flows is something else again.

Before our hurried departure, we did extract from the outfitters a map showing hundreds of lakes like raindrops in the dust. More interested in what Thoreau called the tonic of wildness than in covering distance, we bit off a modest chunk of lakes and joined them with a confident line in heavy crayon. Politely, rapidly, the experts gave us a few hints about finding our way. (There are no markers on the portages, and we were not taking a guide.) "Remember at the first lake you'll see a narrow cut through the reeds; at the fifth don't take the blazed trail but go on to the beaver-flow, then at the next dam bear left through some dead snags. . . . This one straight up the cliff is a bit tricky. . . . But you'll find your way all right. . . . It's really simple. . . . Have a good trip!"

The first leg was a long tow by motorboat up Basswood Lake to the head of navigation, which saved a day or two of dull paddling. By dusk we were at the north end of the lake, and across the line into Canada; a short paddle (we hoped) from that first portage leading out of the reeds. Rain squalls blew up while we pitched the tent, but a white-throated sparrow, symbol of numberless happy holidays, sang reassuringly from the pines, and the loon's wild cry drifted over the water. Before we fell asleep, the big drops were striking with a sharper and sharper *ping*, as wet ropes shrank and the thin fabric tightened like a drum. We were on our own.

Our best trips, we find, invariably start in confusion and rain. This one was no exception. The rain came first, and hard. For a whole day we had the elemental problems of keeping dry and fed, as we cooked with wet wood and a frying pan fuller of rain water than bacon fat. The confusion came the following morning when a hint of clearing weather sent us off in search of that first portage. We drew a blank, and again a blank. It *must* be here. But it wasn't. Would we spend ten days paddling round and round the same lake? Not until we had hauled over two beaver dams (unmentioned by the experts) did we find an old blaze, footprints in the mud, a trail. Here began the first of some twenty portages, ranging from a few rods to half a mile, which led my wife to inquire from time to time whether

6))

this should be called a canoe trip or a walking trip carrying a canoe.

Eventually we learned to guess, from the configuration of the land, where the portages were likely to be. We were able to lift searching eyes from shoreline and compass long enough to appreciate the beauty of the pink granite cliffs, spotted with reindeer moss and lichens; the white canoe birch against dark spruce; the tall red pines (so different from the white pines in the chunky pattern of their needles against the sky); the king-size water lilies described in 1823 by Dr. Bigsby, first artist of the border-lakes country: "Superb . . . about the size of a dahlia . . . double throughout, every row of petals diminishing by degrees, and passing gradually from the purest white to the highest lemon-colour." Among the lilies suddenly appeared a young buck, antlers in velvet, watching us with more interest than fear. Ospreys—and once a bald eagle—soared overhead. Every lake had its welcoming committee of loons, calling their greetings and laughing at us when we got lost.

For we did get lost, through a bit of spectacular stupidity that cannot be explained away by saying that we were portage-drunk. I simply forgot a lake. It was a round, featureless little lake in a chain of five, but it threw us off count. (Incredibly, neither of us could remember how many portages we had made that morning.) For an hour or two that tiny, nameless pond was to us as important as Lake Superior.

Moments like this, amusing in retrospect, serve better than weeks in a library to give you an understanding of what the early explorers and *voyageurs* were up against. Look at an eighteenth-century map of these lakes. A series of vague shapes, compounded of rumor and legend, strung

8))

on a river of hope. Floating upon this river with its treacherous rapids, upon these lakes with their quick, uncertain squalls, a frail birch-bark canoe, loaded to the gunwales with ninety-pound bales. Two or three bales made a load on a portage—and a portage might be several miles long. Indians, some hostile, some friendly, but the friendly ones forever seeking the White Father's aid on the warpath against their neighbors. Look at the French explorer Vérendrye, wounded veteran of Malplaquet, devoting his life and the life of his four sons to the service of New France, rebuked by the corrupt Minister of Marine at Versailles for being so dilatory in discovering the Western Sea! How many of the thirty-six portages from Grand Portage to Rainy Lake, or the twenty-six from Rainy Lake to Lake

Winnipeg, would that foppish official have endured—the Partridge, Big Rock, Caribou, Fowl, Moose, Big Cherry . . . on, and on, and on?

For portage fatigue there is no cure like an island. The island that we chose, in a many-armed but little-traveled lake, could stand for any of a thousand others in general cast of its features; its expression, its smile of welcome at the end of a back-breaking day, was its own. Too small to be shown on the map, it was perhaps a quarter of a mile long and half as wide. We spotted our camp site from far across the lake; an open grove of pines near the southwest tip, with sufficient level ground for a tent and sharply sloping rocks that promised deep water for swimming. Coming closer, we identified the green masses along the northern shore as low-bush blueberries. The core of the island we found to be a tiny sample of apparently virgin forest: towering red and white pines, a few canoe birches, poplars, small spruce and arborvitae; underfoot the moss and ferns and springy, crumbling debris of the primeval forest floor.

On this peaceful island occurred, a day or two later, the Battle of the Reflector Oven. Though we had thitherto ignored them successfully, these ovens, the outfitter had impressed upon us, are essential. Time came for the test. The oven was drawn up close to a bright active fire, the batter was in the pan. My wife promised herself not to look at it for ten minutes. In ten minutes, it looked exactly as before except that the surface was covered with a fine gray ash. Ten minutes later no change, except that a number of small bits of charred wood had joined the ash. The tears in her eyes were half smoke, half frustration. Finally, with the rashness of ignorance, I started a roaring blaze, a proper conflagration that was lapping around the oven and contents within seconds. We both stood spellbound as the cake drew a deep breath and rose up, up, up, brown and beaming before our enraptured eyes. The forces of light and heat had triumphed.

As all this was going on, unruffled by the holocaust, confident of crumbs while yet the sparks flew upward, appeared the boldest bird of the north country, the Canada jay or whisky-jack (from the Indian *weeskaijohn:* "he who comes to the fire"). "It is a noisy, familiar bird," wrote the geographer David Thompson, "always close about the tents, and will alight at the very doors, to pick up what is thrown out; he lives by plunder, and on berries, and what he cannot eat he hides; it is easily taken by a snare, and, brought into the room, seems directly quite at home; when spirits is offered, it directly drinks, is soon drunk and fastens itself anywhere till sober."

A variety of mammals—from fussy little red squirrels to black bear and moose—give life and color to the border-lakes country, but only one gives it shape. This is the beaver's domain. Evidence of his work was everywhere along our route. He had formed some ponds and raised the level of others. Newly felled trees floated at the water's edge, their foliage still green; old snags showed where the water level had been raised years ago. Chips lay on the ground, as neat as if cut with an axe, but marked with the slightly concave imprint of the beaver's chisel tooth. Beaver houses and beaver dams, enduring fabrics of interwoven logs and twigs, showed the amazing strength and technical skill of the animal that was, in the last analysis, responsible for our being in that country at all.

For it was the fur trade that first lured the white man into the northern wilderness; and beaver, of course, was the heart of the trade. The silent, V-shaped ripple that we see crossing the pond at twilight; the resounding slap of the broad tail on the water as we are discovered—these are today almost synonymous with a north-woods vacation. Yesterday they were strictly business. Thirty thousand beaver pelts were shipped in a single year along the great

canoe highway which eventually became the official boundary between the United States and Canada.

Of the countless residents of the north country, our favorites were the loons. Open any scientifically arranged bird book and you will find the loons up front, as the most primitive birds, nearest to the reptiles from which they sprang. Edward Howe Forbush, the great New England ornithologist, considered that of all the wild creatures in that region "the loon seems best to typify the stark wildness of primeval nature." Its mad, quavering, human cry is among the most poignant notes of the outdoors, evoking an almost painful awareness of man's kinship with earlier—and perhaps more permanent—forms of life. One associates it with the plaintive inquiry of the whitethroat, the ecstatic certainty of the hermit thrush, the strident clamor of the Canada goose, and the first faint, hesitant announcement by the spring peeper that the earth's sleep is not the sleep of death.

Grounds for divorce differ according to state laws. But there are certain remarks, when made by a fisherman's wife in time of stress, that would be universally recognized as sufficient by any judge who has ever wet a line. As with libel, the truth of the remark is not necessarily a defense. Several days have passed since the Battle of the Reflector Oven, and supplies are dwindling. By now fish are more than a source of sport; they are a supplement to corned beef and Spam. It is dusk; there is just time for a few more casts before the light fails and the mosquitoes, dormant during the day, make their brief, fierce evening sally. Suddenly I am into a heavy fish. I have already taken a twelve-inch bass on the same plug, but this is something bigger. There ensues a sharp struggle, interspersed with terse commands to the bow paddle about keeping the canoe off the rocks. Finally, after consummately skillful maneuver, I bring the beast near enough to be identified as a fine northern pike. I call the glad news and reach for the wire leader to haul him in. At that precise moment, from the other end of the canoe, comes the devastating remark: "Oh . . . pike . . . aren't they very bony?"

They are. And it was.

Inch by inch that crayon line drawn across our map a week ago had undergone a metamorphosis, changing from intention to experience. Past the halfway mark of our roughly circular route, we were headed back toward Basswood Lake and home. Our canoe glided beneath the famous Picture Rocks: "High precipices of shattered granite," as Bigsby described them a hundred and thirty years ago, "beautifully striped downwards by broad bands of white, yellow, red, green, and black stains"; decorated with Indian drawings of unknown antiquity, still depicting today in bold vermilion the animals that were here before the white man. This last leg of our twelve-day trip drew us continually to the past, for here we were on the historic canoe highway, now the well-marked Boundary Route, which found us one minute in Canada and the next in the United States, depending on the current of the river or the location of a portage. The portages were no longer between lakes; they were around rapids. The roar of falls generally preceded our first glimpse of white water. Both contrasted sharply with the quiet, static quality of the ponds and bogs and beaver-flows we had left behind. Paddling up the Basswood River, headed roughly southeast, we could almost believe, as did the early explorers, that we had but to turn our bow around to reach in time the mythical Sea of the West and the northwest passage to China.

Our concern with these waters was a less serious one than theirs, yet it wasn't wholly frivolous. We were searching not for new lands or untrapped beaver, but for recreation in the original sense of the term. The two or three parties we met in the wilderness were on the same trail. "I should be pleased," wrote Thoreau, "to meet man in the woods. I wish he were to be encountered like wild Caribous and Moose." Not easy; but in a roadless area the concept becomes less fantastic.

CHAPTER 2

Three-Mile Portage

O U R wilderness trips do not, as I said, assume a passion
for discomfort. Yet they do occasionally involve a degree
of effort that would be scarcely tolerable in different circumstances. It all depends on where you are. If someone
asked me to carry a canoe on my shoulders from Washington Square to Central Park, and then walk back to pick up
a forty-pound knapsack and bring it over the same course,
I should feel put upon. The equivalent distance on a forest
portage trail—where the footing is somewhat more precarious than a Fifth Avenue sidewalk—may be viewed, if not
with equanimity, at least without despair. It is a matter of

16))

the context. For one thing, there are fewer appropriate diversions on Fifth Avenue. Even if I were John Kieran, I couldn't hope to flush a ruffed grouse at the base of the Empire State Building (though I have picked up a live praying mantis there), or pause to eat blueberries in front of the Public Library, or find moose dung where the trail crossed Rockefeller Plaza. But I anticipate. The portage I have in mind came near the end of an eight-day canoe trip through the central part of Algonquin Provincial Park in eastern Ontario. Less remote than the Quetico-Superior area, it is also a hillier country, with small swift-running streams and long carries between some of the lakes.

The history of the region is instructive. A hunting ground of the Algonquin Indians, and later of the Iroquois, it was bypassed in the western explorations of Champlain, who makes only casual mention of the area. An early map identifies it merely as "Grande chasse de cerfs et de caribous." It is naturally a forest region; the thin soil will support trees, but not agriculture. Before the lumbermen arrived in the 1870's, the eastern part of the park was covered with a splendid stand of white and red pine, of which a few patches still remain; the western part, by sugar maple and yellow birch. Despite the promises of the land-development companies, efforts to farm the cleared land were doomed to failure. A few farsighted individuals realized that the forest cover of this high country was a vital protection to the watershed of the rivers that flowed out of it. And so, happily, since there was no more quick cash to be made by private exploitation, in 1893 the area was preserved as a park "for the use and enjoyment of the people." Nowadays, along the highway which cuts through the park's southwest corner, it is used to the limit; there is scarcely room for the wash lines between the tents. Yet, twenty miles and a dozen portages away, we had managed to find complete solitude and a true sense of wilderness.

By the time we reached the three-mile portage we had been in the woods for a week. After the first two portages, the outboard motors had been left behind. One outboard can shatter the peace of an entire region; it is as appropriate in a wilderness area as a motorcycle is in church. Wilderness is, of course, an elusive concept, yet no less real because it is difficult to define. The Wilderness Act puts the idea quite eloquently for a legislative document: "A wilderness, in contrast with those areas where man and his own works dominate the landscape, is hereby recognized as an area where the earth and its community of life are untrammeled by man, where man himself is a part of the natural community, a visitor who does not remain and whose travels leave only trails."

By that definition, we had reached something like wilderness the third night out, with three lakes and a stretch of river between us and the populous campgrounds. Darkness had threatened to catch us in an area of mosquito-ridden flats and cattail marsh after an exhausting series of short portages around rapids of which we had long since lost count. We had been forced to camp on the only dry ground in sight, a steep hillside where no one in his right mind would have attempted to pitch a tent. The only "trammelings" in the vicinity—reminding one of faint cowpaths in a precipitous Vermont pasture—had apparently been made by moose, and the only creature to have altered the landscape was the beaver. Our own travels had been by canoe and trail, and as visitors all we asked was to remain on the hillside long enough to get some sleep.

Partway up the slope I had found a suggestion of level ground among the roots of an old white pine, and by digging and scraping had made room for our two air mattresses, terraced one above the other. It may not have been a room at the Ritz, but it served, and there was a certain pleasure in sleeping where surely no one had ever slept before. The only safe place for a fire was the narrow strip of shingle at the water's edge. As we were eating our supper, half standing, half leaning against the bank at our back, we glanced up to see a five-point buck quietly watching us from the marshy flats to the eastward. In the low rays of the setting sun—that theatrical light which gives such depth and texture to a landscape—his coat was an incredibly warm, deep russet. Looking back on that evening, I can think of worse places to be benighted.

Now, four days and several long lakes later, we were encamped on an island, in a grove of great white and red pines, of hemlock and cedar and balsam fir and scattered paper birches—obviously one of those bits of virgin forest that had escaped the lumberman's axe. Directly opposite us on the map a dotted line led away from the lake, marked "por. 242 c."—which means a portage of 242 chains, or approximately three miles. It also meant that our trip was almost over; yet we still had ahead of us its longest and most memorable day. (Memorable days are those during which you keep asking yourself, "How did I ever get myself into this?" and answer yourself, "Anyway, it will be fun to remember.")

We were up at dawn, after a night in which the full moon had emerged from a silver cloud in a scene that not a

thousand kitchen calendars could spoil, and the loon calls had sounded eerier than ever by moonlight. No ray of sun had yet penetrated to the forest floor; we should have to cook breakfast in the damp shade and strike the tent still heavy with dew. But before I had pulled up the first tent peg, the lake was already alight with a bright blanket of incandescent mist, on which floated, apparently some feet above the surface, a boat-shaped island with a single windblown pine for a mast.

Reminded inevitably of a Japanese painting, I realized how true it is that, as art historians have pointed out, we see landscape in terms of man-made pictures. A beautiful view is quite literally "picturesque." Every grove of big trees is compared by somebody to a Gothic cathedral. Vice versa, however, how many tourists see the soaring columns of Notre Dame in terms of the forest that originally inspired them? Hundreds of paintings of English parks have given us a taste for tidy, manicured landscape, down to the postage stamp of lawn outside the suburban picture window; but until very recently in the long history of Western culture, wild nature has been abhorrent. The Olympic rain forest has not yet had its Constable, and the sea of grass that once covered our prairies will never, alas, have its Turner. Now that outdoor photography has become one of the fine arts, the cultivation of our taste for wildness may henceforth depend more on the camera than on the brush.

Partir c'est mourir un peu applies to leaving a wilderness as well as to leaving a friend. When you are literally pulling up stakes and folding your tent, you are aware of how swift is the transition between anticipation and memory. That earlier night on the hillside already seemed far in the past. Today was to be our last full day in the woods, and according to the map it would be full enough. A three-mile portage, when you have to go back for your knapsacks, means a nine-mile walk, and there would be at least one stretch of paddling and a shorter portage on top of that. And as yet we weren't even at the beginning of the long portage trail. Hefting the three knapsacks to be sure that the weight was evenly distributed, we stowed them in the canoe and spread the tent to dry in the sun. The water now was glassy calm, in pleasant contrast to the first leg of the trip, when the lakes were covered with whitecaps and the north wind, funneled through the connecting river valley, almost ripped the paddles out of our hands if we failed to feather them.

Even under the best conditions, with a compass and adequate map, one cannot—or, at least, I cannot—always head straight for a portage. From a few feet above the surface, a canoeist can no more see all the convolutions of a lake than a newborn caterpillar can visualize the whole leaf on which he nibbles. This time, however, it was easy. Though the mouth of the river by which we expected to find the spot was entirely hidden in underbrush, there was an obvious opening nearby, among the big trees, and when we landed we could hear the murmur of the invisible stream. Bits of the trail having been flooded by beavers and only recently made passable again, the portage was little traveled, and we had been warned against getting lost in a maze of abandoned lumber roads. However, it doesn't take a Daniel Boone to tell when a trail has been walked on, even if there is no mud to show a heelprint. Not far from the landing we noticed the broken tip of a fern and a wildflower crushed to the ground—enough to show that someone had been through not long ago, since neither was wholly faded.

Three-Mile Portage

As usual, I carried the canoe the first trip across. Walking with a canoe on your shoulders has its pros and cons. The human frame best accommodates weight bearing straight down, as any Jamaican woman can tell you; I would much rather carry a sixty-pound canoe over my head than a fifty-pound knapsack on my back. And as you pick your way along a log or from stone to stone on a muddy stretch, the canoe almost seems to help you to keep your balance, like the long rod of the tightrope walker. But under a canoe you are a horse with blinders *and* a sunbonnet; the view is strictly straight ahead and down. In these circumstances, a narrow twisting trail is a nightmare, with trees dreamed up by Arthur Rackham reaching over to sideswipe your burden as you go by and knock you off balance. After a while your collarbone begins to ache, though this is no great problem if you have a fixed yoke bolted to the gunwhale; the pads slowly shape themselves to your shoulders as a shoe shapes itself to your foot. When you want to rest, you keep your eye out for a convenient limb or a narrow V between two trees, where you wedge the bow with the stern on the ground and so slip out from under your shell.

For a middle-aged desk worker with no Algonquin Indian blood, a pattern of fifteen minutes' carrying and five minutes' rest seemed about right. Like bicycling and mountain climbing, canoe toting unearths muscles you forgot you had. Here a little advance conditioning helps. A clergyman friend of mine who likes to take his vacations in the mountains makes a practice of carrying a packful of rocks up and down the stairs of the parish house for a fortnight before he sets out. Visitors who drop in on parish business while this is going on may be momentarily puzzled. So, perhaps, were my neighbors when they saw a canoe wandering

around our pasture each morning before train time, like a snapping turtle looking for a place to lay its eggs.

But on the long portage, I blessed every minute of those dry runs. Our first rest, to be sure, came early; we were barely on our way before we reached the site of an old lumber camp and paused to sort out the grown-over roads from the proper trail. The grassy clearing was sweet with the smell of ripe raspberries in the sun. An abandoned lumber camp is like a frontier fort in a long-forgotten war. A few earthworks remain to remind one of the former scene of carnage, but the fosses are mostly filled in, and the dusty parade ground is long since clothed with green. If one can forget the great trees that fell in the battle, an open area like this has a charm all its own.

As we rested, I recalled the particularly attractive spot where we had spent the second night of our trip. After a morning's upwind paddling and a rather rough passage through the outlet of a lake, with the waves piling up in the shallows, we had come to a smooth stretch of water above an old dam of giant moss-covered logs. Rising through the lush grass of the nearby clearing, like half-sunken hulks in a harbor, were the ruins of bunkhouses and stables, surrounded now by sizable second-growth spruce and fir, some of them perfect specimen trees that managed to come up through the heavy turf apart from their fellows, in the manner of field pines on an abandoned New England farm.

Here were sun-loving butterflies and common field flowers strange to find in a wilderness: meadowsweet, yarrow, devil's-paintbrush. Being an "edge" where environments meet—water, meadow, brush, forest—it was rich in bird life, from the myrtle warblers that were feeding on a hatch of fly a few inches above the water to the swifts sweeping far overhead. Every snag seemed to have its olive-sided flycatcher, and cedar waxwings darted about the clearing; but if there is one bird that I shall always associate with this spot—indeed, with this whole trip—it is the white-winged crossbill. We had heard the trilling song of the crossbills from the canoe, and now we watched them flocking amid the treetops as they fed on the cones, the males bright spots of rosy red in the evening sun. The trees themselves were in gentle motion, and I thought that with a little practice one could learn to identify an evergreen simply by its action in the wind: the white pine dances, the spruce bows stiffly from the waist, the cedar merely nods its head. These trees could never replace the noble forest that was cut down several generations ago, but they made one realize that the most ruthlessly exploited land, like the family fortune to which it perhaps gave rise, can become quite respectable with the passing years.

The five-minute rest period was up; time to stop speculating and get cracking. Soon after we left the clearing, the trail began to mount slowly, then leveled off on higher ground. When finally it began gradually to descend, we figured that we must be about halfway across. The trees here were larger, but like the lumber camp we had recently left, they reminded me of an earlier part of the trip when we had seen the same thing on a much grander scale. En route to one of the remoter lakes, we had entered a mature forest which was a world apart from the second growth of the lumbered area. The trees here had survived for the simple reason that it did not pay to cut them down. They were hemlock, a wood far less valuable commercially than white pine, or even than spruce and fir. The tall, branch-free trunks stood well apart, though the tops met to weave an almost sunproof canopy far overhead. Here and there a grove of paper birches made a white accent against the somber background, and we noticed one gnarled maple of huge diameter. But the hemlock allows few intruders, for this is one of the most shade-tolerant of the conifers, and the understory, above a carpet of checkerberries, consisted almost exclusively of its own seedlings, ready to fill the space whenever one of the parent trees crashed to the ground. In this noonday twilight, we met a raccoon who seemed more curious than perturbed at the encounter. Scampering up a tree beside the trail, he stopped to peer around at us through his black mask, with an enchanting expression that, as I think of it now, brings the whole scene suddenly into focus.

This country, however, like the border-lakes country to the west, belongs not to the coons but to the beavers. They have shaped its history: for the sake of beaver skins the Iroquois Indians had once seized the area of the present park from the Algonquins; an eighteenth-century map describes it as "Chasse de castor des Iroquois." And the beavers are still shaping its local geography, as we were to discover today a mile or so further along the portage. They had recently dammed a nearby brook, and part of the old path was now under water. Fortunately, a new trail had been hacked through the alders a few days before we got there, but it was a slippery and squishy business. Once my wife fell flat; by a delicate balancing act we got her upright again with knapsack still in place. Maneuvering the canoe was like driving a trailer truck through Threadneedle Street in a London fog.

Back at last on the old trail, we sensed that we must be getting near our goal. There is nothing quite like the sight of a new lake at the end of a portage. Make the portage three miles, and you are Balboa discovering the Pacific. Moreover, though it may have been prayerfully anticipated, that first glimpse of deep blue through the trees always comes as a happy surprise. My wife was walking ahead, since she had no canoe to cut off the view. "I see it," she said. No sweeter words were ever spoken.

We were, of course, only a third of the way. As we started back to fetch the other two knapsacks, we had that queer floating sensation that comes when you have just shed a heavy weight; walking was practically a rest. Landmark by landmark the reel unwound, a good deal faster this time; the beaver pond, the deep woods, the lumber camp, and finally the lake we had already left so reluctantly, to which we were now saying a final farewell. Here were our knapsacks, presided over by a whisky-jack; he waited impatiently while we ate our sandwiches and left some crumbs for him. Finally came the last crossing of the now familiar path. Though it was curiously difficult to remember just how far along we were at every stage, we seemed to get to the end very quickly.

The long portage over, we still had to find a place to camp. Once more we loaded the canoe. A short paddle, another easy carry, and we were on the shores of a third lake, where a grove of great red pines led down to a sandy beach, above a blanket of blueberries so thick that you could milk a cupful without changing your position. In a sort of trance of tiredness I put up the tent and cut firewood, plotting each axe stroke to hit the wood and not my hand. Later, heartened by rum, gorged on blueberries, feeling almost guilty that there weren't more people to enjoy both, we hung the food pack on a high branch out of the way of the bears, who, I am glad to say, had obviously been gorging them-selves before we arrived and would doubtless continue to do so long after we had gone. Nothing, we thought, makes one feel more a part of the natural community than sharing one's berries with a bear. It was a warm farewell to the wilderness.

CHAPTER 3

By Canoe to the Heart of England

I MAGINE paddling your canoe through a Constable landscape.

The start of a canoe trip is always a magic moment, but
I can remember none more full of promise than that precarious July launching in the Thames above Oxford. Precarious because neither my wife nor I felt at home in our
tippy, well-laden craft; we hardly dared wave back to the

Oxford don and his wife, so helpful in getting us off, so sure that we were going to capsize. The heavy wooden canoe was strange. So, in fact, was the whole idea. One associates a canoe with the wilderness, with escape from man and the man-made. This time we sought the opposite. Like anyone who has traveled in Britain, we'd had provocative glimpses of its vast network of old canals, of those long gaily painted boats laden with coal, or converted for holiday cruising. Obviously a canoe could go wherever a "narrowboat" could, and many places where it couldn't. We had chosen that lovely part of middle England where the Oxford Canal and the river Avon border the Cotswold Hills.

Port Meadow, the ancient Oxford town common, was dotted with black-and-white Holsteins and little brown ponies; the spires of the university receded in the background. On the opposite bank a row of huge poplars lined the towpath. A pair of swans shepherded five mouse-gray cygnets, one parent at each end of the long line. A heron, close cousin to the great blues of our native Concord River, rose lazily from the shallows, and during a sunny interval we heard the song of the skylark. We should have put it on tape; we were to have no more lark weather for ten days.

Early that morning, my wife, looking at the cloudless sky, had remarked happily to the chambermaid at the Mitre on the pretty day. "Well, yes, it does look nice *now*, mum." She knew. By ten o'clock it was raining. We had set out between showers; now they were closing ranks to produce a steady downpour. (As I said, all our best trips start in the rain.) Above King's Lock, whose brilliant flower beds are the pride of the lock-keeper's wife, we turned off into a narrow passage through the reeds known appropriately as Duke's Cut. Instantly the broad, civilized Thames vanished. We felt shut in and strangely remote, and for a moment were back in that winding channel through the reeds in the Ontario lake where, on our first wilderness trip, we almost got lost before we began. Today the route was clear; instead of a beaver dam and a faint blaze on a tree, we came to a narrow, untended lock (the first of scores we were to operate by ourselves) and a neat sign reading: OXFORD CANAL.

Duke's Cut is named for the Duke of Marlborough, but it might well commemorate another duke whose enterprise, coupled with the genius of an engineer, two centuries ago changed the face of England. In 1759 Parliament passed "An Act to enable the most Noble Francis Duke of Bridgewater, to make a navigable Cut or Canal" from his coalpits at Worsley to Manchester. A woman, as usual, was indirectly responsible. Disappointed in love, the Duke had deserted London society to apply his vast fortune to the wild scheme of canal building. Luckily, through such men as Josiah Wedgwood of pottery fame, he met a brilliant engineer named James Brindley. Together they persisted in the face of doubt and ridicule, and of appalling construction problems—tunnels and embankments and aqueducts—and within two years of the passage of the Act, the first boatload of coal was towed through the completed canal. It had been proved possible, and the canal-building boom was on. Thus in the Midlands was woven that web of water that would draw together and nourish the infant industries of Britain. Obviously one of the first necessities was an umbilical cord joining the Midland cities—Manchester, Birmingham, Coventry—with the Thames. So, happily for idle boatmen like ourselves, the Oxford Canal is one of the oldest and by the same token most beautiful. Its embankments are faced with the same sandstone that lends such charm to Cotswold villages. It does not, like many later canals, run straight and dull between big cities, but like a placid river follows the winding contours of the land. Now as we left Duke's Cut and headed north on the canal proper, we knew only vaguely what lay ahead, but we had the essential equipment for a holiday excursion: good maps and few commitments. At the Map House in London's St. James's Street, I had bought the appropriate ordnance maps, known to every reader of English murder mysteries (you'll find one in the glove compartment of the low-slung Bentley) and surely the finest of their sort in the world. Scaled one inch to the mile, they show every hill and valley, every road and footpath, every river and canal and lock and weir and—convenient for our purpose—almost every pub. Luggage was simple: a five-by-seven tent, food for the first few days, bottled gas for cooking, a few semi-respectable garments for big-town stops, raincoats, rain hats, and a rubber sheet over all. By wilderness standards, where every ounce counts and you take it with you or do without, our load was heavy and disorganized. And our plans were amply vague. Like the early canal builders, who respected the contours of the land, we asked only for freedom to follow the contours of the day.

Before leaving Oxford we had obtained from the office of the British Waterways a travel permit for "canoe—with use of locks." It's one thing to be permitted the use of a lock, and another to use one. But we soon caught on to the drill. Where the canal is climbing, it goes like this (with my wife in the stern, and me on land): Shut top gates, crank up bottom "paddles" or sluices (to lower the water level in the lock), open bottom gates, canoe enters lock, shut bottom gates, drop bottom paddles, raise top paddles, wait four or five minutes for the lock to fill (this was my favorite part), open top gates, jump back in, and you're off. The paddles are cranked up with a "windlass," a tool like a tire wrench which is issued with the travel permit; the gates are operated with simple leg power applied, by shoulder or rump, to the end of a massive wooden sweep that balances the gate itself. The canoer's eye view of this routine is rather dramatic: the entry into a long, narrow watery grave with dripping, moss-covered walls rising two stories above you, your view limited to an oblong patch of sky; the heavy thud behind you as the gates close; the wild rush of water as the top paddles are raised; the slow levitation into the light, the new landscape at your resurrection.

We soon found that a canal, like a river, will take you places you will never see from a highway, and that a canal is even better than a river because your eye is level with, or even above, the surrounding country. In either case you are not merely an observer speeding by. Sometimes you can be a source of information. The maintenance man clearing the towpath rests for a moment on his scythe: "Did you see the *Water Rat* below the bridge at Twyford?" A boat, unlike a car, is part of the landscape (some canal boats are bright additions to it) and a tent is a home if only for a night. You meet the farmer whose land you camp on. (You'd jolly well better; the one time we failed to, he appeared with a gun at half-cock.) Your tent pegs give you the feel of the local topsoil; your reception, the feel of the man. We found that there is no one more hospitable than the English countryman—or countrywoman—if you take your time and give him a chance to make the generous gesture.

Never on setting out in the morning did we know where we should sleep that night. The first week's lodgings

went like this: (1) "bed and breakfast" in a canal-side cottage (the bed just vacated by the son of the family who works nights), (2) under a bridge along the towpath, (3) a tent in a mowing, (4) a guest house in Banbury, (5) a sheep pasture, (6) a pig farm, (7) the Crown Hotel in Warwick. Of these, the bridge was the one least likely to be listed by Duncan Hines.

"The law," said Anatole France, "in its majestic equality forbids the rich as well as the poor to sleep under bridges . . ." If a law exists in England against sleeping under canal bridges, I am confident that there are few second offenders. Aesthetically the bridges on the Oxford Canal are superb: stout but graceful arches of weathered stone or brick, no two quite alike, varied occasionally by a tiny wooden drawbridge of Brindley's original design. They are merely crossings between pastures for sheep and cattle. The bright yellow lichens growing on the inner walls might have warned us that a stone bridge makes a damp bed. But tonight in rain too heavy even for unpacking the tent we chose the only sheltered spot in sight: the shelf where the towpath went under a bridge, eight or nine feet of level ground between the inner wall and the water's edge. Bats flitted in and out as we cooked supper. A curlew wheeled and dipped, with wild cries. " 'Tis the place, and all around as of old, the curlews call." Our bridge was no Locksley Hall. But apparently it was the local trysting place, as witness the two girls who appeared just after dark, startled at finding a middle-aged couple in residence, and followed in a moment by their equally startled swains. Hours later their returning footsteps inches from our heads showed that they had not been wholly frustrated. Nor probably more weathered than we, since our bridge proved a wind tunnel. By dawn we knew that, unless we were to grow lichens ourselves, we would somehow manage henceforth to sleep under a roof—be it cotton, thatch, or tile.

I said that we didn't make plans but I take it back. On our ordnance maps we learned to search for the letters "PH" where the line of a road crosses the blue ribbon of the canal. The principal use of my watch was to strike a

"PH" within the midday business hours of twelve to two. (The English countryman, of course, has a built-in chronometer which brings him automatically to the threshold of the nearest public house at the stroke of noon.) A country pub is more than a bar, it is a state of mind and a nourishment to the soul. It is a club without dues, a community center without committees. Here old friends meet daily but strangers are welcome. Our canoe was a sort of guest membership card to the club. "Fancy you two flying all the way from America to do a trip on our cut!"

Nowhere did we get a warmer welcome than at the George and Dragon near Fenny Compton. Here we left the canoe at the pub while we thumbed a ride in a fish lorry (the buses being on strike) to the nearest town for supplies; and here it was that the proprietor forced upon me his treasured copy of L. T. C. Rolt's *The Inland Waterways of England*, with an autographed picture of the famous Joseph Skinner of the *Friendship*, reputedly the last narrowboatman in Britain to be using a mule. Two days later, while I was sketching beside the canal my wife called out. A mule was coming round the bend. And so we met Mr. Skinner and his wife, and in a moment had traveled back two centuries. As they worked the *Friendship* through a lock, he fed a pan of oats to the thirty-year-old mule, and we admired Mrs. Skinner's gleaming brasswork in their snug cabin behind the load of coal. Their vessel had changed little in design since the Duke of Bridgewater's day. Owing to restrictions of the narrow-gauge canal locks, the dimensions of a narrowboat are as fixed as the dimensions of a sonnet. Cargo space most of its length, cabin in the stern, it is approximately seventy feet long and seven wide. One boat fills a small lock; two abreast, a large one. The diesel engine has generally replaced the horse or mule and two boats frequently work in tandem, the power boat towing the "butty." But not all is utility. The pride of "the gaffer and his missus" (he steering the power boat and she the butty) is the rich painting on stem and stern and cabin, the decorated water pot and stool, the polished brass and lace-work within. The traditional painting motifs—roses and diamonds and castles with mosque-like turrets—probably originated with the gypsies. It is a pleasant shock to meet a load of coal in such gay dress, as if one were to encounter a mural instead of a number on the side of a Northern Pacific boxcar. And pleasant to find canals still in commercial use. For the early canal boom had been followed by a bust. They couldn't compete with the railways, which eventually bought them out and frequently let them rot. Today, since nationalization of the railways, they are operated by British Waterways, under the British Transport Commission, which encourages pleasure cruising to supplement the freight traffic. Our canoe was contributing sixpence a mile to the support of the system.

Between Banbury and Fenny Compton the canal had climbed in twelve giant steps to "the summit" at Clayton Top Lock, on a level with the tip of Banbury church steeple. Then came eleven enchanted miles of lockless pad-dling. "Remote, circuitous, utterly peaceful," Robert Aick-man, founder of the Inland Waterways Association, de-scribes it. "Wormleighton and Marston Doles: they are the places in which to forget the modern world. You see a farm house; then half an hour later you see it again, equally near or far, but in the opposite direction." The pastures, with their flocks of sheep and fat dairy cattle, are bounded by dense thorn hedges, teeming with tits and wrens and countless other birds that find them perfect cover. The farmers measure distance in terms of fields: "You'll find a spot for your tent three fields on." It is a gentle land. Old—but age alone does not bring serenity to a countryside. In the Western Hemisphere, land that isn't still virgin is likely to have been ravished. In England nature has apparently never been something to be conquered. On an island too small for wasteful dalliance, the farmer learned ages ago to love and to cherish the land with which he lives in holy wedlock.

. . .

((39

Entering the Grand Union from the Oxford Canal is like entering a highway from a country road, the impression heightened by a huge "road sign" at the junction. As we turned west toward Warwick, we met a stiff headwind, and decided to play the mule. Attaching forty feet of light rope to the bow, one of us walked the towpath while the other steered. For the one it was like flying a kite, for the other like sailing. By mid-afternoon we were sail-striding through the factory district of Leamington, with appropriate comment from the local urchins; in another hour we had arrived, tired and bedless as usual, in Warwick. What appeared like a waterside tearoom, with bright painted doors and flower boxes along the embankment, turned out, in characteristic English fashion, to be a coal wharf. And characteristically the manager emerged from his office to see what he could do for us. In a matter of moments our ship had a safe berth, we had a soft bed in a hotel, and—before we left town three days later—we had several new friends.

As it approaches Warwick, the Grand Union Canal crosses the river Avon on a massive stone aqueduct. There is no official connection between the two waterways. But we were able, by snubbing our long rope around a tree, to line the canoe down the steep and slippery incline into the river. The previous afternoon we had scouted our route from a window of the Great Hall of Warwick Castle, quietly discussing currents and portages in the river directly below us as the guide pointed out the ancient armor and the headman's axe. Now we slipped beneath the chains designed to thwart larger craft and returned the salutes of the tourists hundreds of feet above us in the same window. I doubt that there is a better way to sense the sheer mass of a medieval fortress than to glide beneath its walls in a tiny open boat.

Man made the canals but God made the rivers, and even the well-tamed Avon showed the difference. The neat towpath was replaced by ragged banks and great overhanging trees; patches of reeds higher than your head reduced the channel in many places to a narrow corkscrew. Families of moorhens, the downy young like tiny purple chicks, skedaddled before us in alarm, mallards rose like rockets, wood pigeons flapped heavily from the oaks. Instead of dead water between locks, a lively current carried us along, broken only by the weirs at old mill sites, where we had to portage or slither barefoot down the slippery stone. River travel has no sharp edges; scene flows into scene. The little spotted fawn in the deer park of Charlecote Manor, startled, as it nurses its mother, by the strange object drifting through the nursery. The gristmill with its huge water wheel slowly turning; within, the grinding roar of the millstones, the open sacks of tawny flour, soft to the touch. The golden, gently sloping fields of wheat and barley, the rich green pastures, the red Hereford bullocks, the black-faced sheep. At water's edge the gnarled, pollarded willows (whose withes are still used for basketmaking); the ubiquitous fisherman, sitting on a big hamper full of his elevenses and lunch and tea, motionless as the willows themselves, eyes fixed on his tiny float, occasionally hoisting out six inches of silvery roach or tench. The three pretty, buxom women in print dresses with bright kerchiefs on their heads, barefoot, their felt slippers on the rock behind them, squealing with delight as they netted tiny "tiddlers" and put them in a fruit jar. "For bait?" I asked. "No, love; just for the game."

. . .

((41

The idyll was rudely interrupted at Stratford. Here the Avon, lined with caravan (trailer) camps and public baths, is as quiet on a summer afternoon as a logging river in a spring freshet, with excursion boats forcing passage through a jackstraw tangle of mismanaged skiffs and weaving punts, none having any apparent relationship to the Bard. Below Eversham it becomes broader and deeper, and thereby hangs a heartening tale. Don't forget—as if you could!— the name of Wyre Piddle. Here in an old mill we found the riparian headquarters of the Lower Avon Navigation Trust, an amazing organization of boating enthusiasts who are repairing the locks and, stretch by stretch, making the Avon once more a truly navigable river. Their membership, we learned at the club bar that night, includes practically every occupation except parson and undertaker. But then they all looked young and very fit.

From the Wyre Hill Club to Tewkesbury, where the Avon flows into the Severn, was one long day's run, perhaps fifteen miles, with three locks and two thunderstorms. By late afternoon we were standing beneath the great Norman arches of the Abbey, by evening we were having a beer at the historic Bear, with the principal narrowboat-man in the Midlands. He offered to take us on down the Severn, an unexpected extra dividend to a trip that we thought was over. Farewell to the Avon, farewell to our canoe. From here it would go back to Oxford by rail. Next morning I paddled it to Shakespeare's Boatyard, and left it for shipping in the competent hands of Mr. William Shakespeare.

An hour later we were basking in the bow of a silently gliding narrowboat, blessedly inert after those weeks of hard paddling and lock tending. Surely this was the crown-

ing hospitality in our planless progress. While the *Mercury* went slowly through the Gloucester locks, we slipped off to visit the great cathedral, then rejoined her for the trip down the Gloucester and Berkeley Canal. An attractive but businesslike waterway, it is as straight as the Oxford Canal is tortuous, handmaiden not to the hills but to the sea. Countless old "swing bridges" opened before us; as the afternoon wore on we met heavy-laden seagoing tankers, their decks almost awash. The salt in the air, the gulls perched on the posts along the towpath, showed us that we were approaching the Bristol Channel. Westward we could see the broad reaches of the Severn Estuary. Our trip was

almost over. But as we sat in the sun plotting future voyages
—longer ones perhaps, in longer, drier boats—we knew that
our concern with the canals had barely begun. We had
traveled only a tiny fraction of the inland waterways, but
already far enough to know that they lead straight to the
heart of England.

CHAPTER 4

The Olympic Wilderness

O U R next trip took us, not across the Atlantic, but all the way across our own continent, as far west as one can go in the United States south of Alaska. I had been reading a book about the Olympic Peninsula. "The trouble with this country," I read, "is that it's a damned paradise. It's a standing invitation for people to go out and do something healthy and get deep into trouble." We weren't looking for trouble but we did want a look at Olympic National Park, a largely roadless area the size of Rhode Island containing the world's greatest temperate zone rain forest. Here a rugged mass of snow-clad peaks rises above the mountain meadows, whence glacier-fed torrents drop down to the twilight forest. Obviously our explorations this time would not be by canoe, but on foot along the open slopes and shadowed trails.

Like the previous trips, this one was starting in the rain, which was only proper in the circumstances. Between showers we pitched our tent on a carpet of moss embroidered with wild strawberries. A few yards from the opening rushed a milky, gray-blue river; we could hear the eerie groan of rocks grinding together under water. Beyond, silent and incredibly tall, stood the rain forest.

The Olympic Peninsula, at the core of which lies the park, has been one of America's most enduring frontiers. Seattle is separated from it by Puget Sound; northward lie the Juan de Fuca Strait and Vancouver Island; westward lie the Pacific Ocean and, five thousand miles beyond, the islands of Japan. Why did the Olympic wilderness so long hold its own; long enough for this splendid remnant to have survived commercial exploitation, to be saved at last as a national treasure? Partly isolation, but even more a matter of geography and climate. The coast is treacherous and the harbors few. The lowlands presented early explorers with apparently impenetrable jungle, the highlands with rugged snow-crowned peaks. The first white men settled here only a hundred-odd years ago, and before that even the Indians had kept pretty close to the coastal fringe. The lush forests are a gift from the sea. Warm, moisture-laden air drifting in from the Pacific quickly rises and cools as it strikes the western slopes of the Olympic range, causing the greatest annual rainfall on the North American continent—over twelve feet in the lowlands, an estimated twenty on certain spots in the interior. This, in turn, has two unique and dramatic effects: snow fields and permanent glaciers at relatively low altitudes and a forest growth that has been ap-

propriately described as a "temperate jungle"—how appropriately, my wife and I could not have imagined until we
left the comforts of our tent among the strawberries and
took to the trail.

During the night the loud patter of rain on our cotton
roof had faded till the river's steady roar again took over.
The sky was clear and the woods were steaming by the
time we were ready to start. On entering the average woodland one has a sense of the landscape closing in; whereas
when you step into virgin forest it seems almost to open
out, with long vistas between widely set columns which
disappear into a vague green roof far overhead. The very
scale of this world strikes one with awe. Trees that, sliced
through, could make a dining-room table, rise to the height
of a twenty-story building, swollen at the base with massive,
moss-covered buttresses. Ferns grow at their feet and out of
their elbows; what looks like a vertical branch turns out to
be an independent tree that has taken root in a crotch, high
in the air. From lower limbs hang great beards of gray club
moss. Broad leaves, contrasting with the feathery needles
above them, make a horizontal pattern of green platters
hungry for light. Not here the cathedral-like symmetry of
the coast redwoods; rather a sense of vast columns standing
amid ruins, of fallen shafts and shattered pediments, of
cosmos struggling out of chaos.

The chaos, of course, was only in our heads. Each member of the forest community has its own personality and
highly specialized way of life, from the slimy banana slug
at our feet to the topmost twig fighting for its share of the
sun. Man, who changes what he touches, had touched nothing here. As we set out, avoiding the roots and mudholes,
along the narrow trail that was the only sign of man's pres-

ence, we felt strange yet somehow at home. It was a foreign country, but not a hostile one. The language was different, but an occasional word was familiar. Soon we learned to recognize the four great conifers: Douglas fir, Sitka spruce, western red cedar, western hemlock.

The Douglas fir, dominant tree of the whole Northwest, stood out with its scarcely tapering, branch-free trunk and deeply furrowed bark, suggesting what the "King's pines" of New England, marked with the broad arrow for man-of-war masts, must have looked like to our forebears. Individually, the Sitka spruces were still more imposing, with their massive buttressed bases and huge unfurrowed boles. Found only on the coastal strip, north to Alaska, they reach their greatest size here on the Olympic Peninsula. Later that morning we saw the world's largest, over sixteen feet in diameter. The canoe or western red cedars were even easier to recognize, with their stringy bark, downswept limbs, and trunks like clustered cathedral columns. These are the source of the Indians' dugouts and their totem poles. The ranger station we had just left was shingled with them, weathered a soft gray, and that evening, when we built fires of wet wood, we blessed their kindling qualities. Most familiar to us was the hemlock, whose shade-tolerant seedlings crowded each rotting log, at one spot making a fabulous tree-grown bridge where the parent trunk had fallen across a gorge.

Below the big trees was a tangled understory, broadleaf maple above and vine maple beneath, the latter arching in every direction and rerooting where a branch strikes the ground. Below them in turn grew the sharp-pointed sword ferns and the deer ferns with their antler-like fertile fronds, the sweet-smelling vanilla leaf and the clover-like oxalis.

And everywhere, of course, the mosses and lichens and fungi that thrive on rotten wood and make the whole cycle possible.

Apparently there exists no standard definition of a rain forest, but this is the one used by Franklin D. Roosevelt when the park was created in 1938: "The conspicuous rooting of trees on fallen trees and stumps and a heavy growth of tree moss." Hence the huge buttresses, the trees standing on fantastic stilts where the seed germinated on top of an old stump and the roots crawled slowly down to solid earth; hence the arrow-straight colonnades, incongruous in this random jungle, showing where centuries ago a row of seedlings sprang from one fallen giant. And here too the answer to the lumberman's claim that over-age and rotting trees are wasted: in the true rain forest they are the *only* seedbed; seldom if ever will you find a seedling springing directly from the soil.

Mile after mile we followed the gently rising trail, snaking between the great trunks, fording swift streams where harlequin ducks bobbed in the rapids leading their ducklings and where we found our first water ouzel. We flushed whole families of ruffed grouse—much redder than their cousins in our New England woods—and marveled at the tameness of the blue grouse or "fool hen," which has probably saved many a lost and unarmed man from starvation. But we almost missed the tiny saw-whet owl, motionless on a dead limb just out of arm's reach. As the owl and I looked each other over, I thought of E. B. White's classic reply on being asked if he watched birds: "Yes," he said, "and they watch me."

Five hours and twelve miles later the trail began suddenly to rise in sharp switchbacks from the valley floor.

Hitherto the dense jungle had been broken only by grassy meadows where the elk had foraged. Now we had occasional glimpses of snow-capped peaks. On our left rose sheer rock cliffs, carpeted at the base with maidenhair, most delicate of ferns; to the right the slope dropped off so

steeply that we had a squirrel's-eye view of the Douglas firs, looking straight downward from the top branches, like a sailor at the masthead. The path leveled off, dipped slightly. Something deeper than sky-blue sparkled among the tall trunks. A few more steps and we could make out ripples running over the surface. At the darkest spot, a circle grew and vanished. The lake: and the trout were rising.

. . .

Heaven comes in many shapes and sizes. The heaven of the Eskimos, they say, is hot; the Arabs' is cool, with dancing girls; the Persians' is an ever green garden. But give me a blue mountain lake at the end of a long climb. Frame it with timber untouched by the axe; fill it with brook trout, deep-keeled, orange-bellied, ready to the fly. Let the sun be warm after swimming and let the nights be cold under the stars. If there must be mosquitoes, let them settle down at nightfall. Let the winter wren sing at midday and the olive-backed thrush at dusk. Let the first ray of morning light strike the snow fields of the western peaks; let the long, clear note of the varied thrush announce the day.

A damned paradise. A standing invitation to go out and get into trouble. Next morning, however, we didn't get into anything except some ten-inch trout, which rejected the salmon eggs I had been told they adored and went for standard flies such as the Cahill and Montreal, last wetted in the Adirondacks. With enough fish to eat, we swam, loafed, sketched. Not till the following day did the invitation of those sunlit snow fields become a sort of Olympian command. No mountaineer, I am unstrung by a high ladder or the sight of a child in a treetop; I would sooner sweep a brick chimney than climb a rock one. My wife, on the other hand, is a steeplejack *manqué*, so between us we strike an average. We knew that a trail from our tent led directly to a glacier on the shoulder of Mount Olympus. This far at least we would go.

Mountaineers would call it a walk. Recent rockslides had made a few tricky spots; oddly enough, wild columbine always grew there, a red flag of warning. Patches of dirty, needle-strewn snow became more frequent as we gained altitude. Banks of bright yellow violets gave place to delicate white avalanche lilies. Now the trail became wholly snow-covered. In two hours the woods had fallen behind. We had reached timberline; before us rose a slope of dazzling unsullied white, broken only by scattered rocks and ragged lines of gnarled Alpine fir. Taking off our shirts and digging in our toes, we started to climb, now and then sinking thigh-deep in rotten snow. On every side we could see rivers of melting ice and, with slight qualms, hear them roar deep under the snow we walked on. We stopped often to breathe hard and look back at the peaks which slowly rose as the forest retreated; we had seen all this from a distance, but how different—how strangely detached and peaceful— to feel a part of it!

One last steep climb and we were on the edge of the glacier, looking across at a new world of snow and ice, down into a dirty steel-blue crevasse—all quite enough like the pictures in the books to satisfy two armchair Alpinists. Reluctant to move, but chilled by the wind from the valley below, we considered how to get down. We should, I suppose, have slid on our bottoms, but we had no ice axes for brakes and there were scattered rocks to dodge. An invitation to trouble. I recalled a favorite passage in that classic of British mountaineering, *Unsuccessful But Not Wholly Irrelevant Attempts to Scale Mt. Everest,* in which, on the third and last attempt, "the Leader being at the bottom of a crevasse, Sir Roland Throckmorton suffering from a broken leg, and a native porter having frozen his buttocks waiting for the sahibs to proceed, the situation began to look slightly embarrassing. . . ." So we took the safer way of just leaning back and loping along, our heels dug in.

If we had gone faster, we might not have noticed a sparrow-like bird, with black head and pinkish-brown body, that dashed ahead of us from rock to rock, much like the slate-colored juncos that frequent the bare hilltops of New England. It was Hepburn's rosy finch, "the mountaineer's friend." He was the capstone of our day; if we ever meet him again we'll be back, for a moment, on Mount Olympus. Unless it be Proust's famous *madeleines*, I know nothing so evocative of time and place as the sight—still more the song—of some particular bird. Here in the Olympics, the winter wren's trill conjured up Vermont's Green Mountains. For me the loon's laughter will always be the border-lakes country; the mountain quail is a remote spot above Kern River valley in the Sierra Nevada. That emerald arrow, the European kingfisher, is an old mill on the river Usk; while the yellowleg's "Whew! Whew! Whew!" brings back a Long Island salt marsh of my boyhood, when shore birds were still fair game. And even now when I hear the robin's song for the first time in the spring I am momentarily in a suburban garden where, at the age of ten, I began a bird list, proudly headed ROBIN.

Spring comes late to the mountain meadows. July was almost over when we moved our "base camp" up to a ridge overlooking the whole Olympic range. At five thousand feet, snow still lay on the northern slopes, and the massed wildflowers were just reaching their peak of bloom. As the big trees in the lowlands stagger you with their scale, the mountain wildflowers overwhelm you with sheer color. Acres of it—deep blue of lupines, covering whole hillsides; soft red of Douglasia against dark juniper; flame-red and magenta of Indian paintbrush; bold yellow of wallflower and diffused yellow of glacier lily, pushing its way through the snow; purple of mountain daisy and white of avalanche lily, growing in carpets that obliterate the trail. In the rain forest, colors are muted; there is an oceanic vastness and sameness and sense of hidden life; the great trees seem age-less and time stands still. In the high country everything is on display and happening at once in a frantic rush to get through the life cycle during the few weeks of summer. Within a dozen square yards I found glacier lilies just emerging from a snowbank, in bud, in full flower, and al-ready fading.

Among the trees near timberline another struggle is ap-parent: not, as in the forest, for light, but for shelter. Groves of seedlings grow up in the protection of one old tree; I counted over a hundred fir and cedar in a single clump—so dense that, as the fog swept up the ridge, we felt a cone of warm dry air in its lee. Individual Alpine firs, worn to a scraggy point, spread at the base in wide "skirts" where deep snow protects new growth from winter winds.

The trees must stand and take it; the animals have more choice. With the onset of cold weather, the elk move down from the high country to their winter range in the valleys; the black bear we spotted in a grassy swale was already fattened after his winter sleep; the marmots—heavier, hoar-ier versions of our woodchuck—hibernate for no less than seven and a half months. Now in the warm sunshine they stood at the entrance of their complex burrows and whistled a danger signal as we approached. Easiest to see, particu-larly in the early morning and at dusk, were the graceful black-tailed deer.

For a week we lived in and out of the clouds. Just as we felt that moss must surely be growing on our north sides, the sun would burst out and the nearest bushes would bloom with our steaming socks. At night, snug and warm in our mummy bags, we took comfort in the thought that to appreciate the weather you should live where it is being hatched.

After the forest and the glacier and the mountain meadows, we felt as did the couple in Robert Frost's poem:

> This, *then, is all. What more is there to ask?*
> *But no, not yet.*

There was still the strip of wild Pacific beach, recently acquired by the park, another wholly different environment in this world of contrasts. With the Park Naturalist we drove the ninety miles to the coastal area, took a boat down a long lake, and finally followed the world's slipperiest trail among great hemlocks and head-high bracken and huckleberry and salal (the stuff the florists use in their arrangements) to a roadless strip of coast, where we pitched our tent beneath a spreading fir a few yards from the sand. Again we felt that blend of familiarity and strangeness. Rocky headlands, white gulls against dark evergreens, were suggestive of the coast of Maine. But imagine a beach where the flotsam above high-tide line is a jackstraw tangle of huge logs bleached white and worn satiny smooth; where the sand is crisscrossed with tracks of deer and bear, of skunk and raccoon; and where the ebb tide reveals kelp-covered rocks for a quarter of a mile out to sea. Offshore, instead of low-lying islands, were fantastic towers crowned with trees and sharp needle rocks, shaped like the mesas

and pinnacles of a desert canyon—sculptured by the sea, as the desert is sculptured by wind and sand.

Particularly odd to anyone brought up on the eastern seaboard—but wonderfully convenient for camping—were the streams of fresh water flowing from the forest straight across the sand. Firewood was stacked in all sizes from matchsticks to yule logs. Here and there one saw a huge disk a few inches thick cut from the butt of a big tree and branded with the original owner's code number—evidence that timber rustlers had been at work. And with luck one might spot a ball of colored glass that had once floated a Japanese fisherman's net, crossed the Pacific on the Japan Current, and ended its long journey on this beach.

At low water early in the morning my wife went off beachcombing by herself while I groped my way seaward through the fog to explore the tide pools. In rocky basins pink-walled with coralline algae, I found starfish ranging from ocher to purplish-brown, flower-like sea anemones and cone-shaped "turban-shells," clinging limpets and bright orange worms; feathery weeds and light-green sea lettuce and iridescent ribbons of wrack. Standing on the outermost rocks, the land lost in fog, I might have been alone in the world; only the murmur of surf indicated which way lay our tent, which way Japan.

As the fog burned off under a hot sun, the shrill cries I had heard since dawn materialized into a flock of oyster-catchers, their red legs handsome against the dark wet rocks. Inshore a pair of bald eagles were swooping and diving in perfect unison just over the treetops, like a pair of fighter pilots practicing maneuvers. A striped skunk, indifferent to my presence, nosed among the kelp.

That afternoon, leg-weary, I was ensconced on the warm sand with a sketchbook. My wife came up and suggested a brisk walk. I yawned.

"Why don't you go and be Anne Lindbergh?" (This was just after publication of *Gift from the Sea*.)

"But I've *been* Anne Lindbergh all morning."

So we joined forces again. There were few enough hours left for walking and birding, for squeezing into caves in the rock and exploring around the next headland.

Two nights later we scoured our aluminum plates and watched the sun sink into the Pacific for the last time. We had slept in our tent for almost a month. We hadn't been "deep into trouble." But we had learned afresh the uses of solitude. And we had learned much beside. When not alone we had shared a campfire with men to whom the wilderness is a joy as well as a profession. These members of the Park

Service are themselves a striking testimonial to the values they work for: men with whom John Muir would gladly have climbed the High Sierra or Henry Thoreau walked the Old Marlborough Road, whom the Northwest's own David Douglas would be proud to see among the great trees that bear his name. They represent America's growing awareness that there are times and places in which even a fine timber tree is worth more alive than dead; that, as the late Aldo Leopold put it, "the chance to find a pasque-flower is a right as inalienable as free speech."

CHAPTER 5

Beachcombing in the Virgin Islands

To me, as to most of us, the term "national park" has
always suggested snow-capped mountains, sculptured canyons, evergreen forests, swift-running streams. One certainly doesn't associate it with coconut palms rustling above
dazzling white beaches, with turquoise and bottle-green
oceans, with moonlight on banks of cumulus cloud drifting
before the trades. We didn't, at any rate, until we visited
one of the youngest and most seductive members of the

park family, the Virgin Islands National Park. When we pitched our tent on the beach one morning in early November, it had been officially in existence for less than four years. We were in fact the only campers on the island.

The park comprises about three-fourths of the island of St. John, which is smaller and far less populous than either St. Thomas or St. Croix—the other American possessions in the Virgin Islands group. St. John lies seventy-five miles east of San Juan, Puerto Rico, in the Lesser Antilles. It is about the size of Bermuda, nine miles long and up to five in width, volcanic in origin, the coast a sinuous line of sheltered bays and rocky headlands, the interior a jumbled mass of low mountains rising abruptly from the shore. The climate is benign, with the lowest recorded temperature 68° and the highest 91°, and only five or six degrees difference between summer and winter. Since there is happily no airport on St. John, it is reached by boat from St. Thomas—a half-hour run almost due east (the Caribbean Sea to starboard and the Atlantic Ocean to port), through an archipelago of small islands or keys, in what is surely one of the loveliest approaches to any of our national parks.

The permanent population of St. John, including white residents, amounts to only about eight hundred, largely concentrated in two settlements outside the park area. For non-camping visitors there are various accommodations, including a luxurious resort on the site of one of the great sugar plantations, which is full to the last beachside cottage during the height of the season. And of course there are the old-timers among the tourists who "discovered" St. John many years ago, who have their own favorite spots for winter holidays or who have even yielded to its charm and made it their permanent home. Under increasing pressure from the tourist trade, already firmly entrenched on St. Thomas, the whole island might well have succumbed to "progress" within a very few years if Mr. Laurance Rockefeller had not seen the opportunity to present the nation with a unique national park, where one can step into a wilderness environment hardly out of binocular range of a bikini.

Arrangements for our trip were simple enough. We had sent ahead by air freight our tent and other camping gear; supplies we could buy on the spot. Snorkels and flippers for exploring the coral reefs were the only new bits of equipment. To be sure, before we left home our friends had raised polite eyebrows at the very idea of camping on a tropical island. They seemed to envisage leeches dropping down from the trees and vipers rising from the ground. In gloomy moments they saw us caught some night in the path of the army ants' autumn maneuvers, with nothing left next morning but a few gold teeth, a skillet, and the tent's aluminum poles. What, they asked, about snakes, scorpions, lizards? These hazards proved illusory. No snakes, no army ants, scorpions small and non-combative, lizards everywhere and utterly charming. It is true, however, that I did not quite believe in the whole thing until we were packed up and actually on our way.

Until a few years ago, travel on St. John's few rough roads and trails was entirely by donkey. Now it is largely by jeep. We were lucky enough to be driven to our destination by the Park Naturalist, whose duties, including lectures in the native villages, take him all over the island. The previous winter he had made the first experimental camping trip in the park, and reported back to Washington that it was not only possible but a delightful experience. "Our activities," he wrote, "were viewed by the inhabitants with a mixture of awe, concern, and amusement."

There was no direct road to the spot we had in mind. The route turned out to be in the form of a giant fishhook: a steep climb up to the shank of the hook—the centerline road—along the ridge and down to the farther shore, a backward curve and final climb and hair-raising descent to the remote bay that was our destination. To us every switchback, every pause to look far out to sea or nearby into the jungle, was a fresh page in history, in botany, in the strange new world of the tropics. This was not primeval forest, nor was it a man-dominated land either. It was something else: an isolated spot where civilization—even luxury for the few—had sprouted quickly and quickly faded away, like the ghost towns in California, or those fabulous cities in the Amazon jungle. Here the lifeblood, while it lasted, was neither gold nor silver nor rubber, but the juice of the sugar cane. For over two hundred years after Columbus discovered this multitude of islands and named them for St. Ursula and the Eleven Thousand Virgins, they remained relatively unoccupied. Not till the early eighteenth century did the Danish West India Company establish a permanent colony and build a fort whose ruins still stand above one of the Caribbean's finest harbors. "I have selected a place to build a fort," wrote the governor proudly to his king, "and permitted the planters to indicate which pieces of land they preferred." As one drives through today's jungle, it is staggering to learn that the whole island, to the tops of the highest hills, was cleared and planted—largely to sugar cane —within fifteen years of the governor's letter. From the centerline road one gets a glimpse now and then of an old estate house at the head of a valley, a white dot against the enveloping green. Down by the bay rises a tall chimney that once served the furnaces of a sugar mill. And the road beneath the tires of our jeep—cut into the volcanic rock of the hillside, built up over precipitous slopes with masses of crushed stone—is the same road over which once rattled the mule-drawn carts of cane. How many slaves died to build it is not recorded. They revolted once, and almost captured the island; a century later when slavery itself died out, the great plantations died with it. So the forest, always lying in wait, reclaimed its own.

And what a forest! For a northerner, the combination of infinite variety and close similarity between species made identification a nightmare. Whereas in the Olympic rain forest we felt that we were off to a good start when we had learned the four principal conifers, in the tropics all seemed to be confusion—partly, I suppose, because it was so alien. A great many tropical trees show a baffling family resemblance. Here on St. John every other tree seemed to have narrow "drip tip" leaves for quick shedding of occasional torrential rains, or else long bean pods like our catalpas: one of these is known as women's tongues, since its dried pods rattle in the wind. A few were easy to pick out, such as the kapok with its massive, buttressed trunk and seed pods bursting with the silky fibers that are used for "unsinkable" cushions by American yachtsmen and as wads for blowguns in the Amazon jungle. We identified the umbrella-shaped rain tree with its pink flowers and pods tasting of licorice; the lignum vitae, whose heavy cross-grained wood is so hard it is used for gears; and—most obvious because of its smooth and copper-colored bark—the tree with a name you can taste on your tongue, the gumbo-limbo or turpentine tree. This multipurpose tree not only flavors chicken gumbo, but in the form of fence posts (where it takes root like our willow) it helps to keep the chickens safe for the pot. Here and there along the roadside, rows of gumbo-limbos marked the site of an old property line; later we saw a noble avenue of them on the abandoned road between a former estate house and its mill. By the roadside and in old clearings grow various tropical fruits. We stopped to sample the sugar apple and the sour-sop that grow in abandoned pastures like the wild apples of New England—both edible by man and cattle, and the latter prized for a sort of ice cream made from its pulp.

As we reached the curve of our fishhook course, the road dropped off in a series of switchbacks that would put a goat on its mettle. The vegetation changed as we descended. There is less rainfall on the coast than in the mountains, and the slopes and headlands exposed to the steady trade wind have almost a desert dryness. Barrel cacti along the roadside reminded me of the time we had pitched our tent (the same one now in the back of the jeep) in the Organ Pipe Cactus Monument north of the Mexican border. A moment later I thought I saw an organ pipe cactus itself, but it turned out to be a different species, which branches some distance above the ground, more like a candelabra. Huge century plants, also reminiscent of the Southwest deserts, were silhouetted here and there against the sky. A flock of goats scrambled up the slope away from the road, as the jeep, with my wife and me walking behind, made its last slalom down the headwall to the level of the beach that was to be our home for the better part of a week. A wide strip of shimmering white sand between two rocky promontories, it was crisscrossed almost to the water's edge with flowering vines, including morning glories and pink sweet peas. We pitched our tent in the only shady spot, beneath a spreading grigri tree. The smaller painkiller tree in our back yard insured us against emergencies: for a headache you put a leaf in your hat; for sore feet, in your shoe. (An alternate native remedy for headache is a rusty nail stuck in the hair; respecting the signal, your friends leave you alone and you recover that much faster.) Water was to be had from the cistern of an old building that was being converted into the park ranger station for this end of the island. (Its former uses were indicated by the ruins of the bay rum still that went with it.) In our rucksack was a bottle of Puerto Rican rum, and there were lime trees nearby with fruit ready for the shaking. As we listened that evening to the diminishing rumble of the jeep, we figured that we would make out all right.

In respect to other human beings, we had the beach to ourselves. But I would rather think of us as guests of the permanent residents there. Of these the most conspicuous were the brown pelicans. For them the shallow, sheltered bay, teeming with "fry," was a happy hunting ground. Next day we learned their routine. The earliest arrivals would appear from out to sea, silent and ghostly, at the moment when the cottony clouds at the mouth of the bay were awakening from gray to gold. Slowly flapping and gliding, they would drift in so low over the water as to be almost invisible against the still-dark headlands; suddenly there they were, grotesque shapes growing gargoyle-like from the rock that protruded above the water a stone's throw from our tent. By the time I had taken a quick dip, muttered ritual curses on the midges (who have a poet's

passion for dawn and dusk), and was scooping a hollow in the sand for our breakfast fire, I would glimpse out of the corner of my eye a vertical streak and a splash of white water: the first dive of the day. From then on till sunset, when the last straggler drifted out to sea, it was an almost continuous show. Perched on a rock or a post, a pelican may appear unwieldy; aloft, he is a functional object to delight the heart of the artist or aeronautical engineer. The broad wingspread with the open-fingered primaries, the fan-shaped tail are perfectly designed for slow, wheeling flight. But watch him when he sights his prey. In one swift, corkscrew motion the great beak turns downward, the wings fold back, the head (which has been tucked behind the ample bosom in the manner of a contented dowager) reaches purposefully forward, the feet stream out behind him till finally, in the split second before he hits the water, the whole bird is a living arrow. I spent happy if exasperating hours trying to catch with pen and pencil the various stages in this maneuver.

This first morning, as the sun rose higher and sand grew hotter, we knew the time had come to take a look at the cool underwater world ourselves. Diving we left to the pelicans (neither of us folds up much like an arrow) but we did have face masks with snorkels, and rubber flippers to go on our feet. A dark area of the bay bordering the rocky part of the shore had been pointed out as a coral reef. Approaching as closely as we could on foot, we put on the flippers and masks (an initial feeling of claustrophobia quickly vanishes) and swam toward it. What we expected to see I don't know. What we saw was a new world, in a new dimension.

The first sight of a coral reef is one of life's memorable firsts. Intellectually you have known that this underwater world exists. Friends back from winter vacations have spoken glowingly about it, and you have "oh'd" and "ah'd" in polite response to their excitement. You have read about it in books and seen it (on a far grander scale than you will ever experience) in professional color movies of the life of the deep. Yet none of this prepares you for the moment when you first look through that magic glass, belly-down in the warm, gin-clear water. You feel "like some watcher of the skies/When a new planet swims into his ken"—except that this time you are doing the swimming.

The shapes, the color, the motion—all are strange, yet eerily suggestive of scenery on the earth's surface. Pin-

nacles and flat-topped mesas rise above the level sands of the shallows; farther offshore, canyons plunge into darkness. But the sharp shadows of a terrestrial landscape are lacking: everything is bathed in a soft, diffused light. Coral, though composed of millions of minute animals, is plantlike in its growth. The variety of patterns is bewildering: trees with thick trunks and proliferating branches, others composed of segments that suggest the giant Joshuas of the desert; round grooved boulders of "brain coral," and delicate branching "staghorn coral"; gently waving sea fans, wispy tresses, broad rubbery umbrellas. This weird miniature forest, however, is not the cool green of the woods on land; it is a subtle blend of the warm colors of the palette: red-browns, ochers, subdued pinks and purples. And its beauty is but a background for the incredibly gaudy fish that swim in and out among the branches.

The fish, singly and in schools, are what first catch the eye and hold it in a sort of suspension of disbelief. Here is every shape that can swim: fish slender as a pencil or round as a dish; smoothly streamlined or blunt-nosed and square; triangles and teardrops and flying wings; fish that seem to be all head and others that seem to be swimming backwards owing to the great "eye" painted on their tails, like the eye on the hind wing of a Polyphemus moth. Here, indeed, is color comparable to that of the butterflies and moths: bold combinations of bright purple and yellow, of yellow and black; bodies of coppery red and azure-blue bodies with yellow tails; color in broad vertical bands, in spots, in stripes, or softly blended like the pattern of light from a stained-glass window. And this magic world is ever in motion, some fish "grazing" on the minute algae that grow on the coral, others darting in and out of the caves in the coral rock where they are completely hidden from sight (a tiny fish will drive off an intruder twice his size, like a kingbird harrying a crow), still others cruising slowly along, singly or in schools, indifferent to the clumsy Gulliver sloshing about in their sky. The whole community sways rhythmically to and fro with the slow pulsation of the waves; you see but scarcely feel the motion, for you are drifting with it—drifting over the world of Matthew Arnold's "Forsaken Merman":

> *Sand-strewn caverns, cool and deep,*
> *Where the winds are all asleep;*
> *Where the spent lights quiver and gleam,*
> *Where the salt weed sways in the stream,*
> *Where the sea-beasts, ranged all round,*
> *Feed in the ooze of their pasture-ground . . .*

Friendly beasts, most of them. In the shallows, you have only to watch for the sea urchins, clusters of long, black, poisonous hatpins fixed to the coral rock. Barracuda frequent these waters, but the experts do not consider them dangerous unless (as seems unlikely) you go swimming about with bleeding wounds. Sharks may come close inshore after dark. We swam happily several times in the moonlight till we learned that the natives—who should know—do their swimming by day, when there is no chance of a myopic shark mistaking the calf of a leg for a wounded fish. We saw neither sharks nor barracuda; this did not disappoint us in the least. The largest beasts—and everything looms larger under water—were the tarpon, steel-gray giants cruising slowly among the reef fish, like battleships amid a fleet of bright-colored sailing dinghies. One evening at dusk, feeding only a few yards from shore, they roiled up the water in a terrifying display of power, as schools of jack—sizable fish in themselves—leapt into the air before them.

Though St. John is one of the smallest as well as youngest members of the national park family, it yields to none of them in variety. After we had lived for a few days on the beach, and returned again and again to the subaqueous splendor of the coral reefs, we were ready for the more strenuous business of exploring the jungle at our back, which we had seen only from the comparative comfort of the jeep. Our objective was the estate house and sugar mill that we had spotted from the centerline road. Behind the bay-rum still, and only a few yards from the beach, the trail entered a dense thicket, beneath an enormous raintree glowing with pink flowers. Soon it emerged on a dry open slope along a ridge of volcanic rock, gray where it had been recently split (the Park Service must have been improving the trail) but mostly weathered a warm red-brown. The slope faced east, the hot sun stuck our shirts to our backs, and warmed the water in our canteens. This heat and dryness within a step from the open sea comes as a shock to northerners. Here the coast is dry, the tides are negligible, and the long-growing cacti—as we learned after filling our bare legs with barbed needles—flourish a few feet from the coral reefs.

The path up which we were now climbing might have been a hundred miles from the sea. No, not quite. For below us lay a mangrove swamp, easily identified by its murky water, dyed brown with tannic acid. And right at our feet

were seashells—top shells, mostly, shaped like a boy's wooden top—which scuttled off at our approach. Some of them were as big as your fist, and each contained a hermit crab that had climbed up into the hills to feed on the foliage. Returning once a year to the ocean to breed and cast off their shells for the next size larger, they sometimes roll like loose rocks down the embankment on to the road—a wonderfully efficient if fortuitous way of speeding the trip.

((73

Now and then a dove would explode from under our very feet, like a ruffed grouse in New England woods. We saw the gray kingbird, called pipiri from its song; the thorn-bushes abounded in bananaquits—gaudy black-and-yellow little birds, as bold and conspicuous as our yellowthroats. We also caught a glimpse of a brown, weasel-like creature darting across the trail: the mongoose, a deadly animal which is responsible for the fact that there are virtually no ground-nesting birds on the island. Introduced by the sugar planters to help keep down the rats, it has become a serious pest, whose only predator is the red-tailed hawk.

We had to remind ourselves that most of this wooded area was cleared land only a century or so ago. (Some of the great trees—we saw a spectacular kapok tree in flower—were obviously older than that.) But how quickly the jungle took over as soon as the planters departed! No doubt because the signs are less familiar, the struggle for *Lebensraum* seems somehow starker in these latitudes, where the shrubs, like the well-named catch-and-keep, are so thorny that a man without a machete can travel only along the trails; where the light-fearing termites build tiny tunnels across the open ground and up the tree trunks to their huge swollen nests; where the strangler fig year by year squeezes the life from the forest tree beneath its ever-thickening coils. As we topped the first rise, we saw one old tree that bravely survived all these hazards, with a termite nest high in its branches, a cactus growing out of the nest, and below that a strangler fig reaching its tendrils to the ground. But to appreciate the work of the jungle one has to see it taking over the works of man. After a long descent on a perfectly constructed and still sound road, and a twenty-minute steep climb up the valley wall, we emerged into an overgrown clearing. From the midst of it rose a graceful, almost elegant building that suddenly gave solid substance to what had been merely words on a printed page.

Only the estate house itself was still standing, but one could reconstruct the outbuildings from the pattern of the walls: servants' quarters, stables, kitchen—the last with

a huge oven, door intact, ready for baking. To reconstruct the way of life that went on in the main house was more difficult, though the empty shell was full of murmurs. The architecture was southern plantation style, twin flights of gracefully curved steps mounting to the columned portico, stuccoed brick walls of pinkish white, screened balconies. One corner of the house was half hidden in a mass of color, where flowering vines from the garden had run rampant, and out of the roof grew a fair-sized tree. The front door swung open, banging in the breeze. The footman had left some years ago, but a lizard welcomed us in. The cool green interior walls stopped short of the ceiling to make use of every breath of air. Even at high noon, ghosts were about; I should like to have returned by moonlight when they might have spoken more clearly. I did the next best thing by descending to the cellar, a dark chamber with vaulted ceiling like a crypt, smelling of dust and damp stone. It was utterly silent except for a weird clicking sound, which I later learned was made by a gecko lizard. Broken shutters, empty rum bottles, and other rubbish lay about: debris from the last high tide this family was to know. But what intrigued me was the coffin in the corner. No simple pine box, but the classic hexagonal pattern with sloping cover—obviously a fine piece of cabinet work, and judging from its size, designed for a woman. Why was it never used? When I opened the lid I found a purple lining, the rich tone undimmed by contact with the light and air. Was she at death's door from tropical fever, only to recover? And did the plantation fail before another candidate could be found for this elegant box?

If life and death within the big house can only be conjectured, the source of its precarious prosperity is immortalized nearby on a monumental scale. Down on the edge of the bay, at the end of a broad avenue bordered by shoulder-high stone walls and ancient fig-festooned gumbo-limbo trees, stands the massive sugar mill. Its walls are of rough stone, chinked with bits of brick and mortar, giving a beautiful mottled effect. The built-in cauldrons for boiling the cane juice, the great ovens beneath, the tall white chimney rising like a church spire above the jungle—all are still intact. Gear wheels and rusted tools lie here and there in the grass. Hot and sweating after our walk down from the estate house (the mosquitoes kept us at an intermittent dogtrot), we could imagine what it must have been like to stoke these roaring furnaces, to skim these steaming vats. No wonder the work ground to a halt when forced labor was abolished.

Before returning to our beach we felt obliged to pay our respects to the people who preceded the planters by several centuries, but who left the landscape much as they found it, and whose only monument is a few rock carvings and the name of the sea in which they were once supreme. The warlike Carib Indians had conquered the peaceful Arawaks before the arrival of Columbus. Deep in the jungle beneath a waterfall, less than a mile inland from the sugar mill, we found their curious inscriptions in the rock wall— swirls and spirals and stylized faces—which are presumably connected with propitiation of the spirit of the island's rarest treasure, water. Now in November the fall was reduced to a mere trickle, and the hordes of mosquitoes from the stagnant pool beneath drove us too soon away from a spot that invited contemplation, that one could easily people in the mind's eye with the painted, shell-bedecked Caribs engaged in their sacred rites.

Before sunset we were back at our camp beneath the grigri tree. The sated pelicans were drifting one by one beyond the headlands. Our brief exploration of the forest, like our first sight of the coral reefs, had increased rather than dispelled the dream-like quality of our surroundings. Where but in a dream does one cook supper beneath a coconut palm, on a fire of split mahogany? Squeezing a fresh-picked lime into my rum, I felt a fatal bond, not with the ambitious planters or the fierce Caribs, but with the still earlier Arawaks, whose easygoing ways were their downfall. "They spent much of their time in hammocks," one reads, "enjoying the hallucinations that came with hemp smoked in their nostril pipes." Nostril pipes have gone out of style, but you don't really need them on the beaches of St. John.

CHAPTER 6

Isle Royale

THE other island in the park system has been known
to naturalists—and to nearby residents—for many years,
but it has had little national publicity. Isle Royale (pronounced "royal") lies like a huge fossil fish in the northern
part of Lake Superior, in an archipelago of lesser islands,
only a hundred miles or so east of the Quetico-Superior
canoe country. The fish is looking southwestward toward
Grand Portage, Minnesota, famous gathering place of the

((79

voyageurs in the heyday of the fur trade. Between its eye, where there is a small inn, and its tail, where the park boat lands and where most visitors stay, there are forty miles of unspoiled woods and lakes, reachable only by boat and by trail. No automobiles are allowed. This is what attracted us to Isle Royale.

Now on a June afternoon as we flew the length of the island we were higher than the gulls, though an eagle might have looked down on us. The ranger-naturalist sat up front next to the pilot; in the back seat, wedged tightly enough to make safety belts a formality, were the ranger's wife, my wife, and myself. An island in a long lake was just disappearing beneath our pontoons. The map described it as "the largest island in the largest lake on the largest island in the largest fresh water lake in the world." We were over Ryan Island in Siskiwit Lake in Isle Royale in Lake Superior, getting literally a bird's-eye view of the country where we planned to camp for ten days. Below us lay two hundred square miles of roadless wilderness.

There had been a sporting quality in our take-off. When the pilot looked over the total load, including the naturalist's heavy cameras and tripods and projector (he was on his way to lecture at the park campground) in addition to our ample knapsacks, he shook his head doubtfully, finally shrugged: "Either we go up or we don't." Slowly he taxied out into the narrow bay, which was protected from the big swells of the lake, though the water was choppy. As the plane gathered speed and spray, it must have looked like an overfed cormorant trying to take wing. The pontoons hit the wave tops faster and faster, harder and harder. They skipped a beat, two beats; then with a final spine-jarring bang they rose dripping, free. My wife, who had had some qualms about this experiment in aerodynamics, relished every moment. "You can have your jets," she shouted in my ear. "Give me a plane that tells me when it's in the air."

From above, the bony structure of the island stood out sharply in the late-afternoon sun. Down the center ran a rounded ridge, paralleled by lesser ridges, with swamps and long narrow lakes lying in the valleys between. We learned that this washboard surface was the result of ancient lava flows, deposited one on top of the other, later folded and uptilted. The whole island, whose highest point is only eight hundred feet above the level of Lake Superior, was completely covered with ice during the last glacial age and remained submerged after the ice melted, only gradually emerging into the light as the waters of the lake slowly sank to their present level of six hundred feet above the sea. Now, as the valleys extend out into Lake Superior, they become pencil-thin bays and harbors, all running in the same direction, like raindrops on a windowpane. We could see the ridges stretching out for miles as chains of islands, substantial and densely wooded near the mainland, then broken into smaller and smaller slivers till they became mere pinpoints of black rock. A few minutes later, as the plane dropped down for a landing, the scene sharpened into a pattern of fiord-like inlets and rocky promontories crowned with wind-swept evergreens, reminding us of the coast of Maine.

Islands have always had a fascination for civilized man, beyond their intrinsic beauty. Like mountaintops, they have the aura of mystery that goes with remoteness and inaccessibility. But whereas thoughout most of history mountains have inspired dread, and still, to those who know them, inspire reverence and awe, islands have an almost opposite connotation. They suggest refuge and escape, but most of all they promise the blessed simplicity of a self-contained world. From the point of view of the modern biologist, this is not just romantic nonsense. The isolation of an island makes it the ideal environment for biological research: a study area with a permanent fence around it, a laboratory in which the relationships between different forms of life can be investigated free from outside influences. Isle Royale is today such a living laboratory. It was, in fact, so considered more than fifty years ago, when some forms of biological research were still in their infancy. The modern science of ecology—the new natural history, as it is called, that deals with the relation of living things to each other and to their environment—did not rise full-blown like Venus from the foam. But if one had to pick a single spot for its birthplace, that spot might well be this very wilderness. Before leaving home, I had taken from the library a formidable tome entitled *The Ecology of Isle Royale*, by Charles C. Adams, a pioneer work when it was published in 1912. An area that has so long been under observation is particularly valuable for study today. For example, there is a fascinating project under way to determine the relationship between the Isle Royale moose and the timber wolves that prey upon them. No scientists, my wife and I hoped to get at least a fleeting glimpse of these mysteries in the few days at our disposal.

Our camping gear was not very chic, but it was light. No mysteries here, as we frequently tell our non-camping friends, who think there must be some particular know-

how involved. We have, to be sure, learned a few tricks for saving weight. Glass is heavy, so we carry our powdered coffee, Pream, marmalade, sugar, and salt in weightless baking-powder tins, with reliable screw tops and adhesive-tape labels. We use dehydrated potatoes, carrots, fruits, soups. We often take our own bread, to avoid the typical store bread that gets squashed into a shapeless mess after a few hours in a knapsack. Our tent weighs five pounds, including aluminum poles, and we carry lightweight air mattresses. Our sybaritical objective is to achieve the maximum in luxury for the minimum in weight.

This trip began, appropriately enough, on a bleak and rocky coast that suggests the beginnings of Isle Royale itself. Wherever a land is exposed to the full violence of the weather—high winds, cold, fog, driving rain, or spray—one finds a vegetation that exists on the borderline of survival. Most successful are primitive plants such as lichens, which were presumably the first to take hold when the bare rock of Isle Royale emerged many thousands of years ago from the waters of the glacial lakes.

Now, as we stood on the tip of one of the eastward-pointing promontories, bracing ourselves against the cold wind, the scene before us suggested those far-off beginnings: bits of gray-brown volcanic rock projecting above the surface, mottled with black lichen near the waterline and bright orange higher up; here and there a bit of green where moss had found a foothold; on the larger islands, the twisted mass of a few stunted firs.

At our feet lay a world in miniature. Every niche in the rock nurtured some tiny plant. The shallow, boggy basins, twenty or thirty feet across, held whole plant communities; dwarfed spruce near the center, surrounded by

low-lying juniper, blueberries (we found them rather taste-
less), hardy flowers like the little three-toothed cinquefoil,
sedum, ferns, and club mosses. Everything was Lilliputian:
fronds of wood fern, knee-high under forest conditions,
were two or three inches tall; shining club moss a half inch
or less. Here in the struggle for survival the rule was clearly
"Keep low, keep your head down." The spruce trees
spread out in skirts, as they do on mountaintops. The junipers, whose central trunks looked old and gnarled, flowed
down over the rocks like ivy covering a wall.

There is a strange mixture here of the inland and the
maritime. No tide rushes in and out of these narrow fiords.
A fairly deep draft vessel can squeeze through them at any
hour scarcely a boat hook's length from the sheer rock on
either side, perhaps herding before its bow wave a family of
American mergansers, as a canoe does on a river trip. But
the soaring, screaming gulls belong to the sea, and the
waves of Lake Superior, which is over a thousand feet
deep in places, are ocean waves. They pound the rock
with bursts of spray and swirl high up into the crevices
and grind the loosened stones below. Far back from the
present shoreline, half concealed beneath trees and under-
growth, we saw a cave that is believed to have been hol-
lowed out by this wave action in prehistoric times, when
the lake level was higher than it is today.

As we turned inland, the trees became taller and
straighter. We entered the quiet darkness of the spruce-fir
forest, the forest that thrives in the cool moist places of the
earth, that once extended, the botanists tell us, along the
line of the retreating glacier, from the Pacific Northwest
to New England. And here on Isle Royale we had an ele-
mentary lesson in forest succession. The trees among which

we stood were for the most part evergreens; white spruce and balsam fir. This is the climax forest—the end product, so to speak—on those parts of the island most affected by the coastal fogs and cold waters of Lake Superior. But a forest is never static. After a fire or a blowdown, the first trees to take over the freshly exposed areas are not evergreens but fast-growing, sun-loving paper birch and poplar. Once grown to maturity, however, the birch-poplar forest casts a deep cool shade, in which its own seedlings grow poorly but young spruce and fir thrive. So at last the latter take over completely, and their offspring continue to grow up at their feet, maintaining the pure stand of conifers until a fire or other cataclysm lets in the sun, and the cycle then starts all over again.

Early in every wilderness trip there comes a moment of awareness, a sudden sense that you are there. I felt it in the Olympics at the end of our fifteen-mile walk through the rain forest; in the canoe country when we had put three or four portages between us and the last settlement. It is as if, somewhere along the way, a door has silently opened and you have been invited to come in. So I felt as I lay in my sleeping bag two nights later on Isle Royale, at the edge of a remote inland lake. The purest voice of the north country, the wild unearthly cry of the loon, was pulsating through the darkness like northern lights through a night sky. A white-throated sparrow whistled softly. An incongruous note reminded me that I was on an island: the regular moan of a foghorn out on Lake Superior. I knew what Thoreau meant when he wrote of "an infinite and unaccountable friendliness all at once like an atmosphere sustaining me."

There is no antidote for rapture like a broken egg, taken raw. Eighteen broken eggs discovered before breakfast, gumming together the contents of a tightly packed knapsack, will complete the cure. I had noticed a stickiness on the axe handle. Now I discovered that those new plastic egg boxes that had looked so pretty on the store shelf were cracked and oozing from end to end. We had not been so smart about our containers after all. Wiser but eggless, we started out on the short, steep climb leading to the central ridge that runs the length of the island. The woods here were strikingly different from those on the coast, only a foghorn's voice away. The trail led through pure stands of paper birch, beneath which lay a waist-high blanket of thimbleberries, as tempting to the eye as raspberries, but rather sickly sweet to the tongue. Dark clumps of cedar grew here and there on the shaded north slope. The boggy spots were lush with ferns, mingled with the bright green spikes of the club mosses and the tall feathers of the swamp horsetails.

We had covered perhaps two miles when, as abruptly as a new slide on a lecturer's screen, the picture changed. Now we had another lesson in the complex life history of a forest: a lesson this time in the effects of fire. Beneath the dense shade of the birches the ground had been moist and springy, the air cool. Suddenly, as if we had stepped from an air-conditioned building onto the hot city pavement, we emerged into the glare of a recently burned-over area. The dry open slopes were barely covered with scrubby vegetation. Grasshoppers rose crackling at our feet. Blue jays darted overhead; the brushy hollows were alive with song sparrows and black-throated green warblers; but the hairy woodpeckers, the nuthatches, and the brown creepers had been left behind, and the song of vireos and winter wrens was no more.

Next to man and works of man, fire is the greatest threat to a forest. Isle Royale has suffered three major fires in the past hundred years. We stood now on the edge of the great fire of 1936 that burned almost a fourth of the island. But if man-made fires, caused by carelessness, ignorance, or just indifference, are a constant menace to our few remaining wilderness areas, fire itself has always been a part of the pattern of nature. When much of America was covered by a vast canopy of virgin forest, the occasional conflagration started by a bolt of lightning would open up an area to the sun, providing a variety of new habitats, and consequently of living forms. The seedlings of many plants, including the great Douglas firs of our Northwest, need full sun and exposed soil in order to start their growth. To take an extreme case, there are in the West several species of pine whose seeds germinate only when the cone has been exploded by fire.

In many instances, fire is the clue to the character of a woodland. The uniform stand of birches through which we had just passed, where the trees were all approximately the same age, was undoubtedly the result of a fire many years ago. Now, in the clearing, so much more recently burned over, the only evidence of past glory was isolated, arrow-straight boles of great white pines, weathered to a silver-gray, one of them topped by an olive-sided flycatcher, who darted and swooped every few moments to pick an invisible insect out of the air, others by sparrow hawks and cedar waxwings.

Soon we were clawing our way up the last steep slope to the summit of the ridge, where it flattens out to a broad whaleback. And here, at the end of our climb, we found ourselves again at the beginning of the plant story, back to where we came in, so to speak, on the coastal promontory. The top was bare rock, spotted with patches of dark, papery lichen and dry reindeer moss, a region reduced by fire to the first stage of forest succession. Exposed to full sun and warm dry winds, and to wide variations in temperature, it provided an even harsher climate for new growth than the moist, cool habitat of the storm-swept shore. Fire had left a scar that would outlast many generations of trees and men.

Before nightfall we had returned to our camp in the lush woods by the inland lake. A walleye sizzled in the pan, and my hands were scarred from unhooking the less choice northern pike that had kept snatching at our trolling spoon. The family of goldeneye ducks that had dived around and under our canoe had retired to the reeds, but a great blue heron was coming to roost clumsily in the treetops, teetering with outspread wings until he finally got his balance. The loons were calling again from lake to lake. As the light faded, I noticed how the silhouette of the farther shore was enriched by a few ancient white pines—live trees, these, not skeletons—that stood out above the forest canopy, and I thought of the great pines Thoreau describes that once rose above the Concord River, only to fall at last to the lumberman's axe. I was glad I was in a national park.

Our most memorable camp site was at the southwest end of the island, within reach of one of its wildest areas, untouched by either fire or axe. We were on the bank of a shallow, curving estuary connecting a nearby river with

the bay, its shores rich with cattails and marsh grass and tall purple asters. Higher up the slope grew red-osier dogwood, Juneberry, wild sarsaparilla. A perfect base for further exploration. One trail led inland through an ancient forest of mixed hardwoods and conifers: tall firs, massive cedars, and white pines, a paper birch so old that its main trunk was gray and deeply seamed, with no remaining trace of the papery outer bark, and each of its limbs the size of a large birch tree in our New England woods. Where a recent blowdown had let in the sun, we entered a patch of chest-high Solomon's-seal and ate our way through a thicket of wild raspberries. Then, abruptly the trail vanished, and we were knee-deep in ooze, amid the hummocks of a great swamp.

The other, longer trail wound its way for five miles to the northern shore. Halfway along, where the path skirted a broad beaver-flow, we heard an unfamiliar, squeaky call that suggested some kind of hawk—and then a deep rumble that made me think for a moment that I was in a zoo. We froze, our eyes searching the underbrush. Only a few steps below us in the shallow pond stood a cow moose with twin calves. They waded slowly toward the bank, and then, with a few graceful bounds, emerged dripping from the slough, crossed the trail ahead of us, and disappeared in the forest. Farther along, where the water was deeper, we spotted a young bull almost completely submerged, in retreat, I suppose, from the ever-present flies.

At last we reached the lake front and were again struck by the dramatic contrasts of this comparatively small island. Instead of the fingerlike points and island-studded harbors that had welcomed us where we first landed, we now found sheer cliffs where the unbroken land mass meets the full force of the waves, where wind-sculptured evergreens cling to pinnacles of rock like the gnarled pines of a Japanese landscape. At the trail's end was the nearest thing to a harbor on this part of the island, a crescent cove, the beach of which consisted of wave-polished boulders, strewn with bleached and rounded tree trunks that reminded us, though the scale was smaller, of the gigantic forest debris on the Pacific beach strip of Olympic Park.

If you are getting up at daybreak, there is no alarm clock to compare with a few hungry moose. Each morning their splashing awakened us as they came down to feed and then stood around in the shallow estuary like a herd of cows grazing in a pasture. In one sense, Isle Royale has been a paradise for moose, an isolated area in which they are protected from hunting and in which, until about six-teen years ago, they had virtually no natural enemies. But the web of life is not so simple as that. In any natural community, the lack of predators to keep the numbers of a species within bounds can be the greatest enemy of all. So it has been with the Isle Royale moose, whose story is particularly significant because it involves another of our finest, but much maligned, American mammals, the timber wolf.

The story opens early in this century, when the moose began to breed on the island, presumably having crossed over from the mainland on the winter ice. Protected from natural predators, and at the same time confined to a limited area with a limited food supply, they went through a cycle of overpopulation, during which the young trees and other browse on which they feed suffered severely, and subsequent decline, as their numbers were reduced by starvation and disease. The cycle was then repeated, with a second population peak in the late 1940's. But at this point, a new actor appeared on the stage. In 1948, tracks of timber wolves were first discovered on Isle Royale, and there was evidence that they were preying on the overabundant moose. Today the moose population is down again to a healthy level, the vegetation is recovering, and the predator and prey have apparently reached some sort of dynamic equilibrium. The concept of ecology, of the balance of nature, begins to make sense when you stop to think that the seedling tree at your feet may ultimately depend for its life on the existence of the wolf.

One does not, in a few days, learn much about such mysteries. One picks up a fragment here and there of an infinitely complex mosaic, and one gets some idea of how the trained naturalist painstakingly fits such fragments together to make the living picture of the whole. Best of all, one gets a glimpse of the natural world through the eyes of men who have grown to love it, not sentimentally but by hard work and exact knowledge.

My last impression of Isle Royale is perhaps the sharpest of all. The scene is neither deep forest nor wind-swept rock. It is the interior of a log cabin on one of the outer islands, a remote ranger station where we awaited a boat to take us back to the main island. The young summer ranger is out of uniform; he has spent his day off taking us to his favorite camp spot on a birch-clad point nearby. Though off duty, he has an ear cocked for the short-wave radio muttering in one corner of the room. His pretty wife comes to the kitchen table with the baby on one arm; with the other she reaches for the coffeepot, always waiting on the back of the stove. Alone for days at a time, she is never lonely. For both of them, the "unaccountable friendliness" of the forest has made the summer slip by all too fast. She has news for her husband. Last night, for the first time on their own little island, she heard the cry of a wolf.

CHAPTER 7

The Great Smokies

Some places are like some poems; return to them again and again, and each time they reveal new meanings and new delights. Such a place is the Great Smoky Mountains National Park, a unique remnant of primeval America, fifty-four miles long and twenty wide, lying along the spine of the southern Appalachians that forms the border between North Carolina and Tennessee. The Smokies are not tall by western standards, seldom rising much above six thousand feet, but they are among the most ancient mountains in the world and richest in natural life. From the air you see a green-clad ridge, not straight and regular like that of Isle Royale, but sinuous and broken, with smaller ridges going off in every direction, separated by deep valleys and tortuous streams. The inaccessibility of the Smokies until recent times has been their salvation. Like a rock in midstream, they stood virtually untouched by the main current of westward migration. The course of empire took its way through easier channels, and thus a bit of the original forest survived—the finest woods, I believe, east of the Mississippi and the best hardwood stands you will find anywhere.

A park like this is a living museum, whose exhibits change with the altitude and the seasons. In a day's climb one can travel through successive biological zones equivalent to a journey from southern Tennessee to the Canadian border, from the great tulip trees in the valleys to the virgin spruce-fir forests of the summits, where the climate is equivalent to that of the coast of Maine. Our first visit had been in early November—"out of season" in terms of the tourists though not of the trees. The flaming autumn foliage reaches its peak here several weeks later than in New England. On the high divide it was already winter. Icy fogs swirled about the summits, and when the sun at last came out a million ice-covered twigs were turned to diamonds.

In later years we came to know these mountains in other moods. In late April, when the dogwood was in flower on the lower slopes and the high hardwood forest was only faintly washed with green, when bright-yellow trout lilies

and pale-pink spring beauties bloomed along the Appalachian Trail and pine siskins flocked in the spruce tops and
played about our camp site. In May, when we had pitched
out tent between showers near a tulip tree whose upright
orange blossoms shone like candles in the mist, when the
silver-bell tree hung its white pendants in the ceiling of
leaves, while the maroon of the wake-robin relieved the
endless greens and browns of the forest floor. In September,
for a lazy week at the lush end of summer, when the katy-
dids were loud at dusk and I saw alight on a thistle my first
Gulf fritillary butterfly, burnt orange above and silvery
below, a beautiful insect that seemed to embody all the hot
glare of the tropics.

Our most recent trip to the Smokies was in late June, the
best time of year for the famous display of azaleas, rhodo-
dendrons, and mountain laurel. The main objective, however, was not simply to enjoy a spectacle but to immerse
ourselves for a few days in the park's finest wilderness area.
Leaving our car at a park campground, we set out with our
camping gear and enough food for three nights.

As every season has its own personality, so every trail
has its own cadence. The one we followed began to mount
in steady switchbacks straight up from the river valley,
gaining two thousand feet in the first three miles. Through
the dense stand of second growth "poplar"—as the local
people call the tulip tree—we began to catch glimpses of
distant mountains. An occasional mammoth red oak showed
that we were approaching the wilderness area. At length
we reached the crest of the ridge and the trail leveled off

to an easy walk. Through a grassy opening in the forest a less-traveled path sloped gently downward to the spring where we would spend the night. The penciled X on our Geological Survey map became a flow of ice-cold water welling out of a sandy slope, set off by the delicate pink of mountain oxalis and the bright red of cardinal flowers.

((99

Great trees stood all about us: buckeyes and red maples, a yellow birch some four feet in diameter, red spruce rising spearlike through the gnarled hardwoods or stretched out on the ground at incredible length, moss-covered and moldering, seedbed of future generations.

Trees like this do not have lower branches. Before sleeping that night, we had to find a sturdy sapling from which to suspend our food bag out of reach of the bears. In bear country this should be a bedtime routine, like brushing your teeth or putting out the cat. One night at the campground we had suffered a lapse of memory which would have been less amusing if we had already been on the trail. Asleep in our tent, we were awakened by a metallic crash that could mean but one thing: a bear in the food box. We bellowed and waved flashlights; the only response was crunching and stentorian breathing as our visitor consumed one pound of steak, two pounds of bacon, four chocolate bars, two loaves of bread, one pound of cheese, one pound of butter, and—with a particularly offensive slurp—two dozen eggs. The raw eggs, my wife pointed our charitably, would be good for his coat. As he lumbered away he stumbled over a tent rope and shook our roof in farewell.

This time, after dark there was only the sweet descending spiral of the veery's song and at dawn the busy *yank! yank!* of the red-breasted nuthatch. Morning was half over before we said good-by to our camp site by the spring and set out on what is known as a rough trail or manway, to distinguish it from a trail that a pack horse can negotiate. As we entered the wilderness area the switchbacks with their moderate slopes were left behind. Clambering up the hogback, with pauses to pant and rest from our packs, climbing down the crazy ladder of rhododendron roots, we began to sense why the Smokies are considered rugged mountains despite their moderate height, why the homesteader left this country to the hunter and the Indian. If we could not really get into our heads the complex geological history of the mountains, and its relation to the forest all about us, we could at least feel it in our legs.

The mountains as they stand today are the product of erosion rather than upheaval, an ancient plateau carved by the slow chisel of the streams. In spring, when there is as yet no concealing cover of leaves, one sees and hears the waters still at work, sparkling threads at the bottom of each V-shaped draw. In contrast to younger and higher ranges like the Rockies and the Sierra, there is little exposed rock even on the summits of the Smokies, for at this latitude six thousand feet is below timberline. The high lichen-covered boulders in the stream beds, architects of deep pools and shimmering cascades, are said to have broken off from bare rock and rolled down the mountainside in the more violent climate of the last glacial age. But while other areas were actually covered by ice or submerged beneath the sea, this region remained a sanctuary for the hardier trees and flowers, with the result that it is today a botanist's paradise, containing more than one hundred and thirty species of trees.

And here most of our eastern trees achieve their maximum size, thanks to the moist air and an annual rainfall second only to that of the Pacific Northwest. Canada hemlock grows up to nineteen feet in circumference, red spruce fourteen, cucumber tree (a magnolia) eighteen, yellow buckeye fifteen, and so on—greatest of all being a noble tulip tree with a recorded girth of twenty-four feet. Here, as in the Olympics, we have watched the valleys steaming after a downpour or stood beneath the dripping foliage as the sun came out and tendrils of mist spiraled upward through a thousand shafts of light. This smoke-like mist, and perhaps the purple haze which even on fair days may lie along the mountaintops, has given the Smokies their name and much of their subtle beauty, so different, for instance, from the massive jagged outline of the Rockies. Subtle but not mild. In summer violent thunderstorms march along the ridges; we have seen great banks of cloud that appeared to rise almost vertically up one side of the main divide, like smoke from a forest fire, blanketing North Carolina in darkness while Tennessee still basked in the sun.

One such storm, followed by a cloudburst, hit us on a September evening years ago when we were camped on flat land near a river. As water flooded under the ground sheet (I had failed to dig proper ditches), the ropes shrank and the tent pegs began working loose in the mud. Barefoot, I stood in a couple of inches of water, hammering in the metal pegs with a camp axe. A flash nearby, and I saw a blue spark leap from my right to my left foot; I felt as if I had touched a Paul Bunyan electric fence. I decided by now to come in out of the rain. Happily the tent held, the storm subsided, we somehow managed to get a fire going to cook our steaks, and by nightfall were gratefully settled for sleep. It was hot, and the tent flap was open. I was just dropping off when I felt something crawl up my arm and across my face. A pack rat, distinctly damp. I told him to go away. Again to sleep, again the scampering up my arm. At this point my wife, who doesn't like rats—even wild and uncorrupted pack rats—had had enough. Angrily she got out a heavy needle and thread and sewed our front door firmly shut. The rest was silence.

Now as we worked our way down off the ridge, the rumble of an approaching storm mingled with the distant murmur of a different stream far below us on whose bank we planned to camp. Two hours later, under an angry sky, we waded through the swift, icy current to pitch (and ditch!) our tent on a tiny bit of grassy level ground. The first drops fell as the last peg went in. With some old curved roots I fashioned a sort of dome to shelter our fire of driftwood gathered from the stream's edge; it hissed and sputtered but miraculously lived, and its updraft carried off the clouds of midges that had swarmed from the grass.

Above the soporific sound of the creek rose the three liquid notes of the wood thrush, in place of the veery that had sung us to sleep at higher altitudes. A great horned owl hooted twice and was still.

Ducking in and out of the rain, I opened a tin of meat for supper and idly read the water-soaked label: "New beautiful party bag and billfold $2.50 value for $1.00. Get this fashionable new pearl white party clutch bag with matching billfold NOW!" Well, not just now.

As I have said, the toughest days in the wilderness are often those that mean most in retrospect. By our modest standards, the next day qualified. In other summers we had paddled and portaged through roadless canoe country; we had lived for a while with the gigantic rain forest of the Olympic Peninsula. But never had we come so close as we did that day to recapturing the experience that the early explorers described with such mingled delight and awe. From our camp site the rough trail led downstream through a mixed forest of virgin hardwoods and conifers, alternately

following the stream bed or mounting steeply through the tangle of rhododendron. At one point the going got so rough that we had to take off our packs and pass them along by hand.

After a few hours of this, any place where you could put your foot down solidly twice in succession felt like a highway. But at least we had a map, and there was a trail of sorts. In 1787, when the French botanist André Michaux penetrated the southern Appalachians, he depended on Indian guides: "June 14. We continued still having the river first on our right, then on our left; we had to pass over great boulders, straddle monstrous trees fallen across the jungle of shrubbery, where one could scarcely see where to go on account of the density of the thickets . . . This trouble and confusion was increased by the noise of the waterfalls and the crashing on the rocks of the river that we had to ford up to our knees. The savages tore ahead through these streams afoot, or ran along the logs . . . and one of us had always to run ahead to see what had become of them, for there are no trails in those places except those made by bears and occasionally by Indians." In his original journal one hears the voice of the trained European scientist in a strange wild country: "*Ils me conduisirent alternativement par des montagnes et des torrents que l'on appelle Creeks . . . Les sauvages tuèrent un Cerf et tandis qu'ils le dépouillèrent, je visitai les torrents ou je reconnus en abondance la Kalmia latifol. et le Rhododendron maximum.*" Today the *Kalmia latifolia*, mountain laurel, was in full bloom, as it must have been for Michaux, its shell-pink flowers massed along the banks of the creek and festooned over the house-high boulders in the torrent.

Someone is supposed to have asked Daniel Boone whether in all his wanderings he had ever been lost. No, he replied, but he had been bewildered (using the term in its root sense). We were bewildered now as we tried to pick out the trail marked on our map. A right-angle bend was clearly shown, and we found a few old blazes where it should have been, but they soon petered out in the trackless forest. Only slowly did we realize that a new trail had been blazed since the map was printed. We remembered a confusing day years ago in the Minnesota canoe country when we found ourselves paddling up a long narrow lake that obviously was not on the map; all came clear when we reached a beaver dam and realized that the beavers had created the lake since the last survey. More often it is the user, not the map, that is at fault. The trouble, I told myself as I tried to reconcile the trail with the map, generally begins with an *idée fixe:* you visualize a trail turning off at such and such a point, a portage at a certain arm of the lake, and you miss it when it turns up unobtrusively somewhere else. A map, like an Ouija board, can be made to say what you subconsciously want it to say. Keep looking at it, even when you think you know it by heart. And don't forget to note the date in the corner: things may have changed.

As the day wore on and we got deeper into the valley, the forest became more and more impressive. The dense understory of rhododendron, virtually impenetrable till a trail has been hacked through it, gives these untouched woods a strangely park-like appearance. Few saplings grow above this deep green blanket; one's eye travels far among the bare straight trunks of the hardwoods and towering hemlocks. The lowest leaves were often so far above our heads that we needed binoculars to identify them. Accustomed to the cozy woodlands of New England, we felt as if we were in an enchanted country where shrubs are trees and everything grows larger than life size. "The spirit-haunted forest, fairy-enchanted,/Stupendous and endless," as Vachel Lindsay called it, where kittens turned to tigers, pigs to wild boars, colts to gold-horned unicorns, where "The smallest, blindest puppies toddled west . . . And turned to ravening wolves/Of the forest."

The Great Smokies

We saw no wolves, and my *Field Guide to Animal Tracks* omits the unicorn; the cloven triangle in the sand on the riverbank was more likely the print of a deer. There were other signs of hidden life. The deep claw marks on a spruce tree were obviously made by a bear. The "scats" here and there along the trail were harder to identify—either fox or wildcat; even the experts sometimes fail to tell which. Bits of evidence fitted together: those big oval holes we noticed in a dead snag, the loud tattooing that had echoed through the forest, and now the black-and-white feather at our feet. This was the pileated woodpecker, the red-crowned cock of the woods, king of his tribe now that the ivorybill is near extinction. Smaller birds were less elusive: a pair of blue-winged warblers scolded us for coming so close to their nest, as the juncos had along the higher trail; a winter wren, reminiscent of the Long Trail in Vermont, lit up the woods with song; a kingfisher shot downstream with his loud rattle. Yet compared to open and brushy country, with its variety of bird song, we found that a climax forest is a quiet place where life goes on unheard and unseen.

Was our trail also going quietly on forever? Packs were getting heavier, our morning freshness was wilting, and our spirits were sinking with the sun. Would we ever get out of here to send for that party clutch bag? We reminded ourselves that we were not lost, only bewildered, and that we were bound to intersect the main trail if we kept on going downstream. This was, we reassured each other, the only possible answer. The map may have been out of date but the river valley was not. When at long last we emerged from our twisting tunnel onto a clear-cut path running in the right direction, we were vastly relieved to find that our answer checked with the one at the back of the book. Near the meeting of the trails was a dark laurel-bordered pool with sheer rock walls but a pebbly beach large enough for a tent and open to the setting sun. Enough for today.

Two days later, having returned to civilization and replenished our packs, we set out on a final trip to see one of the park's rarest exhibits. The flame azalea, member of the rhododendron family, reaches its peak of flowering the third week in June on those grassy summits of mysterious origin locally known as "balds." Again the long climb—three thousand feet of it; again the feeling of a world apart, but this time an open, sun-drenched world, a high island surrounded by blue-green swells extending to the horizon.

Abruptly from the dark woods we had stepped into a meadow dotted with clumps of blueberry, dwarf willows, and low thickets of hawthorn; we heard brush-country birds: towhee, brown thrasher, chestnut-sided warbler. All about—though densest at the edge of this inverted green bowl—glowed the azalea, head high, ranging in color from deep red-orange through pink to almost white. "The clusters of blossoms," wrote its discoverer, William Bartram, "cover the shrub in such incredible profusion on the hillsides that suddenly opening to view from the dark shades we are alarmed with apprehension of the woods being set on fire. This is certainly the most gay and brilliant flowering shrub yet known."

When we had wandered about and looked our fill, we stripped and lay in the deep grass. We were a bit weary after the morning's climb, but from a distance we must have appeared a lot deader than we felt. A turkey vulture, soaring on the rising air along the ridge, circled us deliberately, tilted his scrawny red head, and fixed us with a hungry eye. He seemed to ponder for a while, turning this way and that to get a better look, then reluctantly sailed on. Not quite; not quite yet.

CHAPTER 8

Alaska: Last Frontier

PRAISE ALLAH," as the Eastern saying goes, "for the infinite diversity of his handiwork." Our national park system, which now extends from below the Tropic of Cancer almost to the Arctic Circle, is singularly blessed with diversity. Two island habitats could scarcely present a sharper contrast than St. John and Isle Royale; nor could two mountain environments differ more dramatically than the mellow, timbered ridges of the southern Appalachians and the ice-bound peaks and rolling tundra of Alaska, which includes the magnificent wilderness of Mount McKinley National Park. "To the lover of pure wilderness," wrote John Muir over eighty years ago, "Alaska is one of the most wonderful countries in the world." It still is. A month's travel and camping, barely touching on its wonders, can at least give you the sense if not the substance of this vast area which is indeed a "country" in its own right. Sheer size becomes here a quality as well as a quantity; distance is a palpable fact, of which you are always aware. Superimpose the outlines of Alaska on a map of the continental United States, placing Fairbanks, the principal inland city, on St. Louis. Point Barrow will reach to the Great Lakes; Ketchikan, southernmost city in the coastal strip, will be in the Atlantic off Florida, and the Alaska Peninsula will cross Texas to the Mexican border. Look at the globe and you will see that Nome lies west of Hawaii, in the last time zone before tomorrow. Most striking, to eyes accustomed to maps crisscrossed with highways, is the virtual absence of roads. That amazing feat of construction, the Alaska Highway and its tributaries, gets you to Anchorage and Fairbanks and northeast to Circle; but it is an artery without veins, a trunk road that has yet to sprout branches. North and west there is nothing. This is America's last frontier. It is not only a joy but a responsibility. Still largely a virgin land, it offers a God-given opportunity to practice the principles of conservation that we have learned elsewhere at such appalling cost.

That irrecoverable first impression of a country is wholly dissipated if one drops into its lap from thirty thousand feet. A jet flight is not so much a journey as a displacement: a ruthless relocation of the body with the spirit left somewhere along the way. We had been well advised to enter Alaska not by plane to Fairbanks or Anchorage, but by ship through the historic Inside Passage, an island-sheltered waterway extending for almost a thousand miles from Puget Sound to Skagway near the border of the Yukon. This is the country of Muir's *Travels in Alaska.* "The island-bound channels are like rivers," he wrote, "the tide-currents, the fresh driftwood, the inflowing streams, and the luxuriant foliage of the out-leaning trees makes this resemblance all the more complete." My wife and I sailed from Vancouver, steaming slowly north and west for four nights and three days, "tracing shining ways through fiord and sound," as Muir puts it, "past forests and waterfalls, islands and mountains and far azure headlands." Hours passed without sight of a human habitation. Bald eagles circled overhead, flocks of scoters skimmed over the water, but the only signs of man were the occasional seine boats fishing for salmon. Here the towns, widely scattered along the coast, are like islands in themselves, oriented seaward: Ketchikan lives on the salmon run; Juneau, the state capital, flanked by mountains to the east, has a total of ninety miles of road, unconnected with the hinterland. As one travels northward the mountains close in on the sea. Great glaciers, white on top and blue along the forward edge of the melting ice—some of them now slowly retreating into the valleys they have molded—give a sense of a land still in process of formation.

Historically as well as scenically, the Inside Passage is the true approach to Alaska. These treacherous channels and churning tide rips were the first—and for some the last —stage in the Klondike gold rush of the late nineties, today lovingly refurbished as a tourist attraction. The ship goes as far as Skagway, docking beside the beach where mountains of miners' luggage were once piled in massive confusion and horses and mules were slung overboard to swim ashore. A bulging city of tents at the height of the stampede, it is now a sleepy village, starting point of the narrow-gauge railway that squirms up over White Pass, graveyard of men and mules. One can still see bits of the old foot trail from the train, and get a sense of the triumph the sourdoughs must have felt when they reached the long lake at the summit. Here they built boats of raw lumber to sail sixty miles to the headwaters of the Yukon River and—if they survived the rapids—on downstream to Dawson and the Klondike. It is proudly remembered that, in 1900, more boats were built on the shores of Lake Bennett than anywhere else in the world.

At Whitehorse we had to leave the sourdoughs' route. The great sternwheelers, which until a few years ago would have taken us down the Yukon, now rot on the bank, their towering pilothouses nesting sites for cliff swallows. Reluctantly, we enplaned for Fairbanks. We had re-entered the air age: "Everybody flies in Alaska." Yet we need not have worried about leaving the frontier behind. Fairbanks, metropolis of mid-Alaska, is a frontier town, a pinpoint of population on an empty map, a supply depot for thousands of square miles to the north and west. Eskimos in parkas mingle on Second Avenue with brief-cased businessmen. It is also an intellectual center, but in a frontier setting. The University of Alaska lies across the Chena River from Fairbanks as Harvard lies across the Charles from Boston, but there are detectable differences between the two. The Boylston Professor at Harvard has the right to pasture a cow in the Yard, but I have yet to see a Harvard biologist build his own log house, or Harvard students cut classes in the fall to lay in their winter's supply—not of debutantes, but of moose meat. Self-sufficiency, yes, but with it a sense of mutual help, given and received, taken for granted: the simple friendliness of frontier life, where least of all is any man an island.

. . .

In their ecological study, *Wildlife in Alaska*, A. Starker Leopold and F. Fraser Darling tell how they were impressed with "the grandeur and magnificence of this vast terrain," and they wondered whether man with his modern technology "was going to be the despoiler or the good steward of this last frontier." Mount McKinley National Park is a unique spot to observe man's stewardship. Comprising over three thousand square miles in the Alaska Range southeast

of Fairbanks, it can be reached by the Alaska Railroad
("Not responsible for train delays because of moose on
right-of-way") or, more recently, by car via the Richard-
son and Denali highways. It is traversed by a single, dead-
end road about one hundred miles long, rising from an
elevation of seventeen hundred feet at the park entrance to
almost four thousand at the highest pass. The rest is wilderness. There are not many trails: if you leave the road, you
walk up the broad river bottoms or over the rolling tundra,
which stretches as far as the eye can see, to the base of the
distant mountains. Few trees obscure the view, either of
snow-clad Mount McKinley or of the animals, from Alaska
moose to red-backed mouse, who unconcernedly share their
ancient heritage with man.

On our first hike through the park we began to get
some sense of what the term "tundra" really means. Prior
to this trip we had only the vaguest idea of it, a hazy com-
posite picture of flat plains ending in ice, summer wildflowers, ducks nesting in potholes and, in winter, Siberian
sleigh drivers throwing the least attractive child to the
wolves. Now the picture became a little sharper. From a
distance the tundra looks like a smooth meadow, through
which one might stroll as casually as a Vassar girl gathering
flowers for the daisy chain. Not so. At every step the
dense, scrubby mat squirmed beneath our feet as if we were
walking on bedsprings. We were, in fact, striding on top of
a miniature forest of trees and shrubs: dwarf birch and
dwarf willow; creeping blueberries and mats of cranberry;
Labrador tea with its spruce-like stem and white flowers;
crowberry and the rough-leaved buffaloberry and succu-
lent sedums. Slabs of upturned sod showed where a grizzly
bear had been scratching for a favorite food, the root of the

vetch (wild pea) or of the saxifrage. Above all—or rather below all—there grows here the delicate branching "reindeer moss" and paper lichen so important to the winter diet of the caribou. We were reminded of the miniature plant communities on the wind-swept rocks of Isle Royale. But in the arctic it is not the gales and icy spray from above that dwarf the vegetation: it is the layer of eternal ice below, the so-called "permafrost." During the brief arctic summers only the top layer of earth has time to thaw; beneath lies a layer of permanently frozen ground. Here only shallow-rooted plants can exist. Poplar, paper birch, sizable willows and white spruce can live where there are four feet or more of unfrozen soil during the summer. Where the permafrost is only two feet down or less one gets occasional stands of black spruce and the sort of scrubby ground cover through which we were now hiking. Curiously enough, the same condition that limits growth of vegetation is also responsible for its very existence. The arctic is semi-arid—Fairbanks has less than twelve inches of annual rainfall, and Mount McKinley Park fifteen—but the short, cold summers minimize evaporation and the frozen subsoil prevents normal drainage and holds the ground water where roots can get at it.

In summer the tundra teems with life. Plump arctic ground squirrels squeaked at us from their doorways, freezing bolt upright before diving into their holes, like the prairie dogs of the plains. These fabulously abundant little rodents are an essential link in the arctic "food chain." Foxes prey heavily on them, and they are an important part of the wolves' diet when caribou are scarce. For grizzly bears they are tasty tidbits; we saw many holes in the hillside, deeper than the torn sods of pea vines, where the bears

had been patiently—and, I gather, often unsuccessfully—trying to dig the squirrels out of their burrows. Finally, they are the main support for the park's greatest bird, the golden eagle. Ground squirrels are to the eagles what rice is to the Chinese. Near the top of one of the passes on the winding park road—may it never be "improved"!—we had made a short climb to look down into the nest of a golden eagle built in a cranny of the cliff, and for an hour we watched and sketched the two black-and-white young whose feathers were still fluffy but whose powerful yellow beaks looked quite ready for ground squirrels. The tundra is also a densely populated nesting ground for birds that we generally see only on migration. Driving through the park during the late afternoon we had found practically every roadside pond occupied: here a red-throated loon, looking in the low light like a plate by Louis Agassiz Fuertes; there a pintail with half-grown young; farther on a family of horned grebes, the adults in their rich nuptial plumage, with several of the tiny young riding on the mother bird's back. Now a soft whistle caught our ear. On the top of the next rise was a golden plover that had made the long overseas flight from its winter home in the Hawaiian Islands. What a strange sensation to meet in the mountains, hundreds of miles from salt water, birds that one always associates with sand beaches or the sea! Shore birds don't belong in trees, but a lesser yellowlegs screamed at me from the tip of a scraggly spruce, and an arctic tern had "buzzed" me so close that I heard the whoosh of his wings as I explored the delta area where both were obviously nesting. Short-billed gulls were everywhere along the road and the gravel bars. And above the rolling tundra, hovering and plunging like a sparrowhawk, was a long-tailed jaeger, startlingly beautiful in form and motion, with his black cap and white throat and needle-like tail—a sea hawk that winters at sea in the Southern Hemisphere.

The rolling tundra is a good place for birding; it is also a good place to get momentarily lost. The smooth rounded hillocks, devoid of trees or other landmarks, blend into each other at surprisingly short distances to make an undulating sea of green. When our route lay through a gully we were as blind as a rowboat in the trough of a wave. However, we had only to climb the nearest rise to get a sight on a distant mountain and lay our course accordingly. Out of the wind we were hot and thirsty under an almost cloudless sky, but we soon came on a stream of ice-cold water running through patches of snow that had survived since winter under the dense shade of the willow thickets—a reminder that in these mountains summer's lease is short. The willow stands were dense because they had been browsed by moose, the tips of the branches torn off in a sort of natural pollarding process that results in thick broom-like growth and—happily for the moose—tends to keep the tender fresh sprouts within his reach. Now at midday no moose were in sight, but we had seen two big bulls the previous evening. A bull moose, God knows, is impressive anywhere, but the Alaska moose is even larger than his brethren to the south. I shall never forget that first glimpse of incredibly broad, flat antlers swaying among the willow-tops: how could any creature be strong enough to carry these around on his head? As the tall forequarters emerged into the open, one had a sense of sheer muscular power in a body that is "grotesque" only if one forgets its adaptation to the moose's way of life, grazing as it does on the highest tree tips it can reach. Later that evening, within camera range of the park road, we had watched another bull belly-deep in a pond, feeding on subaqueous plants, torrents of water cascading from his antlers whenever he raised his head. It is comforting to know that the Alaska moose is one of the great American mammals that is holding its own. Though the species was seriously threatened in the gold-rush days when it was the staple food for miners and trappers, it has, under hunting regulations, come back in numbers and even extended its range. Indeed recent studies suggest that more liberal game laws may be desirable in some areas to prevent overpopulation in relation to food supply.

And this brings up a highly controversial question. Where such overpopulation does exist, should the national parks be opened to hunting? This idea, which has been seriously proposed, may have political appeal and even a superficial logic. If the elk herds must be reduced, why shouldn't someone get some fun out of it? Why not, except that the whole park concept would be shot as dead as the surplus elk. Reduction of herds, when it's necessary, must be done by government employees under official supervision, with proper choice of animals and minimum disturbance of the environment. "Controlled public hunting" would involve special licenses and therefore special privilege, which is surely out of place in national parks. Yet if you turn the public loose with guns in our parks, that priceless live-and-let-live relationship between man and beast will disappear. Those persons who prefer to watch wild animals rather than kill them will be penalized, for the "game" will soon learn to keep its distance. Non-hunters will not dare venture into the woods while the season is on. The parks, in short, will no longer be parks.

Early in our hike we had our first good look at a grizzly bear. He was emerging from a thicket but we were some distance off, out in the open, which was fine. Uncaged and unmolested, the grizzly bear is not a dangerous beast. But he doesn't like to be taken by surprise. We had been advised to whistle, or otherwise politely make our presence known, when walking through the dense willow thickets along the stream beds. Realizing that any whistling on my part would rouse a well-attuned bear to cold fury, I left this little courtesy to my more musical wife. Since this bear could hardly stumble on us, we were perfectly safe, and we could study him at leisure. Compared to the sleek black bears we knew so well in the Great Smoky Mountains, he looked round and woolly, like a huge and purposeful teddy bear. As with most grizzlies in summer, his forequarters and prominent hump were bleached by the sun to an almost straw-yellow; face and hindquarters were dark. (After the fall molt, his whole body would be dark brown.) Unlike most wild creatures, he did not seem particularly alert. Why should he be, since he had no natural enemies—and in the park not even that ultimate enemy, man. Seldom have I sensed more keenly than at this moment the spirit which lies at the core of wilderness philosophy. There is something refreshing to the soul in sharing your place in the sun with a wild animal that neither attacks you nor flees at the sight of you. You feel slightly complimented, as Thoreau did "when Nature condescends to make use of me without my knowledge, as when I help scatter her seeds in my walk." Though we were (I am glad to say) of no immediate use to the grizzly, we could at least accept the basic principle of his inalienable right to his domain.

.   .   .

As I said above, stream beds here serve for trails. In the next few hours we found out why. The "dry tundra" of the high ridges, consisting of matted plants and mosses and even bare rock, is easy walking; the scrub on the slopes is not bad if you don't fight it; but the "wet tundra" of bogs and "niggerheads" and shoulder-high brush is simply hell. We had been told, but we had to learn for ourselves. A mile or so beyond the spot where we had stopped to quench our thirst we reached the bank of the creek near which, some miles downstream, stood the log cabin that was our goal for the night. This was not one of those broad river valleys, characteristic of the north country, that are largely dry in midsummer; it was a swift mountain stream, with a narrow, well-defined bed, thickly wooded islands, rock-strewn rapids, and occasional sand and gravel bars. Fondly hoping to keep our feet dry, we started to follow a well-worn trail along the bank, so neat and clear that we thought it must be man-made. Soon it branched and branched again and finally petered out completely in a nightmarish jungle of willow and alder and dwarf birch: a moose paradise, but purgatory for anything on two legs. We slithered slowly ahead by literally walking in the trees, with unsure foothold on springy horizontal branches, or teetering on the hummocks between them. We could well believe the park ranger who had told us that, though he is a fast walker, he once took twelve hours to negotiate ten miles of niggerheads. So we stumbled back to the creek and waded in, forgetting about dry feet and crossing from gravel bar to gravel bar through snow-melt water up to our knees, turning a blind eye to the tempting trails that led off into we now knew what.

When at length we did pick up a bit of blazed trail

running through a small spruce forest, we knew that the cabin was at hand. There it stood in a grassy clearing, surrounded by a litter of tiny flat-topped log houses—winter quarters for sled dogs—and, well away from the trees, a miniature peak-roofed log cabin held twenty feet in the air by spruce poles banded with sheet metal: the cache, universal trademark of the Alaska wilderness. The grizzly bear is the main object of the domestic defenses in the arctic. He may leave *you* alone, but your food supply is fair game. Before we could enter the cabin we had to remove the "bear door" with which every wilderness structure is equipped: heavy planking with a porcupine surface of six-inch spikes driven through from the back. Similar shutters covered the windows. Even this doesn't always work. Friends of ours who have a camp outside the park returned in the spring to find it a shambles. The bears had consumed everything in sight, though not all of it proved digestible; a stack of pamphlets had gone through with the title still quite legible: *Let's Eat Outdoors!*

The cabin had no defenses against the only wild animal that was out for our blood. In this damp sheltered spot the mosquitoes rose from the grass like fighter pilots in the Battle of Britain. Protected by liberal applications of "Off" we soon got used to them. "How were the mosquitoes?" is the first question you hear if you have been camping in Alaska. The mosquitoes are, I venture to say, holding their own, with no immediate need for federal protection.

The creek down which we had hiked ran through a series of rocky pools a hundred yards from the clearing. Here was my first chance to cast for grayling, which takes the place of trout in arctic waters. Fish after fish rose beautifully to a dry fly, and in an hour I had all we could use for supper—several running to twelve inches or more. They didn't fight so doggedly as brook trout or rainbow of equivalent size, but they were, to our taste, even better eating. We cooked the catch on the cabin's 1911 wood-burning stove and went to bed content. The sky was still light between the spruce-tops, for summer days here are long, but the silence was complete. Looking back over the hours just passed, I felt again that "wilderness" is a positive concept and that wilderness travel is a good deal more than simply getting along without roads, just as peace is more than getting along without war. In outdoor recreation the means don't merely shape the ends, they *become* the ends. Ask any fisherman. And thinking of roads, a jarring question kept intruding itself. Had this obvious relation of means to ends eluded the authorities who have begun to convert the unique and beautiful road through Mount Mc-Kinley Park into a common highway? The present road serves its purposes admirably. Driving slowly, one can stop almost anywhere for an intimate view of a moose browsing, a beaver building his dam, fox cubs playing at the entrance to their den, a golden eagle returning to its nest. This and the magnificent scenery is what most visitors come for. There's no point in hurrying because the road doesn't go anywhere. Why then construct at vast expense a broad hard-top speedway, with shoulders built up above the surrounding countryside, marring the landscape, inviting fast driving, destroying by its very size and design the subtle relationship between the visitor and what he came to visit?

Spiritually as well as topographically, the high spot of the Mount McKinley trip was our day with those two great naturalists, the Murie brothers, among the mountain sheep. To be introduced to Dall sheep by Olaus and Adolph Murie is like being introduced to St. Peter by the Pope. Better, really, since none of us that day felt quite ready for St. Peter. It was a bright windy morning, the air washed by last night's drizzle. Adolph, who conducts his summer studies in the park, knew exactly where the rams were likely to be—knew it, I'm convinced, a shade before they had made up their own minds. He set a course across the tundra and then on up a long draw to the foot of a steep talus slope. We stopped often to identify wildflowers: the low evergreen crowberry, the tall white saxifrage, that delicate deep blue delphinium, the Jacob's-ladder—and several of the twenty-odd varieties of willow. A snowshoe rabbit bounded through the scrub and flocks of redpolls rattled overhead. No sooner were we near the rocks than we heard the clear, man-like whistle of a marmot: there he was upright on a bolder, whistling back memories of the Olympics and the Rockies and the other high free places where we had listened to him with affection over the years. He was an old friend. But a moment later there trotted into view (not bounding like a deer but pacing smartly up the incline) an animal that we had never seen but read about often: the very symbol of the arctic, *Rangifer arcticus,* the Barren Ground caribou. A mature bull, he held his head high as if to balance his fine spread of backswept antlers. His coat was a grayish-brown, lacking as yet the white bib that would appear in winter; but his white hocks stood out clearly as he emerged onto the bare ground. We were lucky to see him, since the spring migration—a spectacle so awe-inspiring that one park ranger said it gave him gooseflesh to watch it—had already passed through. Though small compared with the great aggregations north of the Arctic Circle, a number of caribou herds like the one in Mount McKinley Park survived the indiscriminate slaughter of the early days that has been compared with the slaughter of the bison on the prairies. (Unlike the moose, they have not recovered dramatically under protection, in part because the widespread burning of the range, which actually increases the moose's food supply of second-growth scrub, destroys the lichens on which the caribou depend.) In the complex web of life the Mount McKinley caribou have an important relation to the sheep, as Adolph Murie shows in his classic study, *The Wolves of Mount McKinley*. Browsing on the lower slopes they form a sort of "buffer" between the sheep on the high ridges and the hungry timber wolves.

Mountain sheep are seldom found far from the rocks. The reason is clear. I can't imagine a wolf or any other predator catching a sheep on the sliding shale up which we were scrambling. We climbed in short bursts, more or less on all fours, the wind helping to blow us uphill as we neared the crest. A last hitch and we were over the top. Like a sailboat rounding a breakwater, we were suddenly snug and sheltered, looking down into an enclosed world of rounded hills and flat grassy plateaus divided by knife-edged ridges and sculptured cliffs of bare rock. Behind us the wind crackled with a sound of tearing paper, and the odor of sage was in the air. The green slope at our feet was dotted with the blue of wild forget-me-nots, the yellow of arctic poppies, and clumps of tiny pink cranberry blossoms. Far to the southwest rose the white mass of Mount McKinley, towering over the neighboring peaks as if they were mere foothills: Denali, the Indians called it—"the Great One." For a moment as we lay catching our breath we saw nothing stirring. Then on a ridge opposite there appeared, one by one, fourteen white figures walking slowly in single file. Even at a distance their great curving horns identified them as rams. The horns of the Dall sheep are slenderer than those of his larger and darker cousin to the south, the bighorn. The whole animal gives you an impression of delicate poise and effortless control. He is a pure creature of the mountaintops, unimaginable on any less rugged terrain. Close up, his facial resemblance to domestic sheep somehow underscores this essential wildness. We were shortly able to look a ram in the eye. Following the rooftree of the ridge we had just climbed, we peeked cautiously around a great boulder. From a few yards away an old ram and a young spikehorn stared back at us—alert and curious, but unalarmed. We advanced a few more steps, dropping below the ridge, since sheep like to have the top berth. Calmly they went back to their grazing. Taking the hint, we got out our sandwiches. For perhaps half an hour we and the sheep shared the mountain meadow; while across the valley, as if in happy augury, two golden eagles soared and plunged. Then we decided that we were probably lying between the old ram and his favorite resting place; it was only polite to go. We were content. For this we had come. For this indeed Mount McKinley Park had been founded: to save the homeland of the wild white sheep who have dwelt among these cliffs for untold thousands of years.

We were determined to pitch our tent for at least a few days north of the Arctic Circle. We wanted a glimpse of that vast expanse of arctic tundra that encircles the globe between the northern limit of the forest and the southern limit of the ice cap: a land almost as broad as the sea, and like the sea an environment all of its own. We drove back to Fairbanks, where a professor at the University proposed a splendid if slightly startling plan. Two of his friends were just starting on a voyage in a skin boat up the Noatak River,

which drains several hundred square miles of northwestern Alaska, opposite the tip of Siberia. We could fly to Kotzebue, the "Eskimo capital," and from there get a bush pilot to take us up the river, spot the skin boat from the air, and land on the nearest gravel bar, where we should see the *voyageurs* and, incidentally, deliver a package of reading matter and a bottle of rum. Nothing to it. Our written instructions sounded a good deal easier to follow than most directions to a dinner party in the suburbs. "They will have the only skin boat on the river. . . . Will have a white tent flying two strips of 'Hi-viz' orange fluorescent cloth." What could be simpler?

Now as we peered down from the little four-seater plane (the rear seat removed to make room for our knapsacks) it seemed that our rendezvous had gone awry. Our pilot, Nelson Walker, knew this country as well as the caribou whose trails lay below us in a vast network, or as the Eskimos whose old hunting camps, with their debris of bleached bones and hides, showed up as speckles of white against the soft green and warm brown tundra. We had spotted a cow moose feeding in a pond, and a grizzly who broke into gallop at the sight of this strange bird overhead. But for the last hour we had searched every bend of the river, banking to right and left like a marsh hawk hunting for a mouse. No boat, no tent, no Hi-viz. Nothing for it but to set up camp and await their arrival. Our gasoline was running low, but Nelson, like the true bush pilot he was, had his private cache of five-gallon tins in the willow scrub at a fork in the river. We landed with a series of bumps on the gravel bar where the two streams met. One tin was empty, broken open by grizzlies; the rest as usual were intact, since a single taste of high-octane is enough, even for a bear. Refueled, we flew back downstream to find a camp site. Since the river was high, the gravel bars were short and narrow. Nelson found one that he felt would do; he circled, flew over it once, and came in. It was rougher this time: what his friends call "one of Nelson Walker's controlled crash landings." Safely down, he contemplated several rocks, any one of which might have smashed us up, and remarked in wonder, "How did I manage to miss *all* of 'em?" We promised to clear a proper airstrip against his return. Lightened of its load, the plane rose easily and headed south for Kotzebue. We were alone on our gravel bar, with a hundred miles of elbow room in every direction.

Using rocks instead of pegs for the guy ropes, we pitched our tent well out on the bar where, owing to a slight breeze, there seemed to be more gaps between the mosquitoes. We had wondered about firewood in this treeless country, but found ample piles of willow scrub "driftwood" that had been drying since the spring freshets. I loaded the .30-.30 rifle which I had been persuaded to take along as a last resort against importunate grizzlies, though I much preferred the method suggested by Mamie Beaver, Eskimo lady in Kotzebue: i.e., banging two tin plates together. Even this proved unnecessary. Whenever we left camp to fish for grayling or to explore the tundra, we divided our food supply into several different caches, so that a visiting grizzly might not get it all at once. But the only fresh tracks we found on our return were those of a large moose and a caribou.

And so for a few days we enjoyed a taste of the far northern tundra: the breath-taking vastness, the utter silence, and the sunlit nights. Time came for the plane to return. With loving care we staked out a landing strip— marking each end with white rags—and rolled away the largest rocks.

So silent is the arctic that we were instantly alerted by the first faint hum of the approaching plane. Moments later it swept by, dipped wings in salute, and dropped down softly beside us.

Flying south through scattered showers, we could read

the landscape below us a little more intelligently than before. We carried away some sense of a wilderness whose only limits are the limits of the land itself. We also bore with us a hope for the future which I believe to be founded on fact. No part of the earth today is too remote for exploitation. But in Alaska it must be obvious to every Chamber of Commerce that conservation is good business. More than half the population depends on wildlife resources: salmon, caribou, moose, and—less directly but ever more importantly—on those "lovers of pure wilderness," who will continue to come north in increasing numbers while that wilderness remains unspoiled.

We now realize at what cost we have "conquered" most of our continent. Alaska today offers us something that history seldom affords—a second chance.

CHAPTER 9

Canyonlands: A New National Park?

I T W A S a full moon, and the guests were standing looking out over the area south. And one man spoke up and said:
'This is one of the grand viewpoints of the world.' " This
burst of plenilunar enthusiasm appears in, of all places, the
transcript of *Hearings before the Subcommittee on Public
Lands of the Committee on Interior and Insular Affairs of
the United States Senate* on a bill to create "Canyonlands
National Park" in southeastern Utah, at the center of one
of our greatest wilderness areas south of Alaska.

A national park does not simply spring into existence,
fully armed, like Athena from the head of Zeus; Hephaestus
and his hammer have a job to do first. A new park can be

created, of course, only by Act of Congress. Before such a bill can be introduced, many studies must be undertaken, many questions answered; public hearings must be held, hundreds of persons with diverse and often conflicting interests allowed to have their say. Obviously the initial question is: "Does the area meet national park standards?" In a sense these standards were set by the great parks—among them Yosemite, Yellowstone, Glacier, Mount Rainier—that were already in existence when the Park Service was established in 1916. Later they were defined as: "scenery of supreme and distinct quality, or some natural feature so extraordinary or unique as to be of national interest and importance." There is no question on the part of the Park Service or the Advisory Board (a non-governmental body) that the area surrounding the confluence of the Green and Colorado rivers, now called Canyonlands, meets these standards: "It contains perhaps a greater diversity of erosional features than any other comparable area in the country, and it ranks as possibly the world's greatest exposure of red rock canyons . . . It is of unquestionable national significance." There is, however, a sharp difference of opinion about what sort of park we should have. In fact, the amount of heat generated in this debate seems at first out of all proportion to the issues at stake. Commercial interests are lined up against conservationists, game hunters against park "purists," the senior senator from Utah against the junior senator, the governor of the state against the Secretary of the Interior. The political battle over Canyonlands will remain of interest long after the smoke has blown away because it brings into focus basic conflicts about the proper use of our remaining open spaces. Let us take a quick backward glance at the geography and history of this scenic battleground.

Canyonlands lies at the heart of what geographers call the Plateau Province; a dry, elevated plain that in Mesozoic times was a great loop of the sea, and now includes most of Utah, parts of Wyoming to the north and Colorado to the east, and to the south the Grand Canyon of Arizona. It is a country of clear air and sharp edges, of utter stillness and sudden violence. In his biography of John Wesley Powell, who first mapped the area less than a century ago, Wallace Stegner describes it as "scenically the most spectacular and humanly the least usable of all our regions." Indeed, it is so rugged and so difficult of access that parts of it remain unexplored to this day.

Climatically as well as scenically, Canyonlands is a country of extremes. The temperature range is 130 degrees. Rainfall is sparse; what little there is comes largely from thunderstorms and runs off in flash floods. There are virtually no roads; travel is by horseback, foot, or jeep. Indians lived here in the distant past (when the rainfall was obviously greater than it is now), but the first organized exploration was made by the Powell Expedition of 1869— an incredibly daring venture led by that one-armed veteran of the Civil War who was later to found the Geological Survey and shape the entire development of the West. The very year that the railroads were joined with the driving of the Golden Spike, Powell had three specially built boats transported by flatcar to the town of Green River, Wyoming, where the track crossed the Green. Leaving the newly built railroad, Powell and his companions literally plunged into the unknown, through roaring rapids in which they often capsized and sometimes almost perished—to emerge eventually, sunbaked, sandblasted, and half starved, in the calm waters below the Grand Canyon. In the course of this and the subsequent expedition of 1871 they recorded impressions of the Canyonlands country with the eloquence of near disbelief: "Nothing was in sight but barren sandstone, red, yellow, brown, grey, carved into an amazing multitude of towers, buttes, spires, pinnacles, some of them several hundred feet high, and all shimmering under a dazzling sun. It was a marvellous mighty desert of bare rock, chiselled by the ages out of the foundations of the globe; fantastic, extraordinary, antediluvian, labyrinthian, and slashed in all directions by crevices; crevices wide, crevices narrow, crevices medium, some shallow, some dropping till a falling stone clanked resounding into the far hollow depths." Or to borrow a phrase from Ebenezer Bryce (describing what is now Bryce Canyon National Park): "A hell of a place to lose a cow."

The visitor to Canyonlands today can see what Powell's men saw, virtually unchanged. And one attraction of this area is that it can be approached on several levels; from the rim, from the lower benches, from the canyon bottoms, and from the river. My wife and I planned to explore the canyons by jeep, but we decided to take a hawk's-eye view before we took the view of the desert mice and the ground squirrels.

We began with the "grand viewpoint" referred to above, one of the few spots in the proposed park now accessible by road. The two-hour drive was a primary lesson in geology and desert ecology. Nowadays, in the light of incontrovertible geological evidence, one accepts the amazing fact that this weird landscape is the product of erosion: that the principal canyons have been created over eons of time by the slow rising of the earth's crust while the river, maintaining a constant elevation, slowly cut through the rock, as a fixed buzz saw will cut through the log that is pressed up against it; while smaller streams, rain, and frost have ground away at the exposed surface. It is harder to realize that this process is going on now, just as it always has. "When thinking of these rocks," wrote Powell in his journal, "one must not conceive of piles of boulders or heaps of fragments, but of a whole land of naked rock, with giant forms carved on it . . . all highly colored . . . never lichened, never moss-covered, but bare, and often polished." Here is a land ancient without the patina of age, a supremely articulate landscape whose very clarity challenges us to interpret its secrets. The color of the rock is, of course, one key to its origin, though it varies with different exposures. From where we stood we could see the difference between the "white rim" of hard rock and the softer red rock beneath. The former was deposited by the wind, as one can still see from the delicate tracery of matted curves and whorls of what is aptly described as a "frozen sand dune." The red rock was formed by water deposition when all this country lay under the sea. This difference in hardness results in undercutting of the canyon walls; where erosion has proceeded further it has created gigantic mushroom-like columns.

On this dry, wind-swept plateau we found the vegetation sparse. The principal trees—piñon pines and desert junipers—tend to be widely scattered; the latter, often no larger than shrubs despite their great age, are gnarled and contorted beyond belief. Sparse sagebrush on the flats give the landscape here and there a faint wash of blue-green, and yucca with its spikes of creamy-white flowers reminds one that this is indeed semi-desert. But the most striking evidence of desert conditions is the leaf structure of what we think of as broad-leafed trees. The single-leaf ash, the curly-leaf mountain mahogany; their leaves, designed to allow the minimum evaporation, are almost as narrow and tough as the needles of an evergreen. Here was living proof —though barely living it seemed—that evolving forms will develop some way to use every niche in the environment.

On the way out we had met a cowpoke, new style, driving a pick-up truck with his horse in back. (The modern cow pony enjoys this form of locomotion, and is as eager to go for a ride as the family dog.) Ignorant of the country, he was scouting ahead to find water for a thirsty herd of cattle. We could tell him there wasn't any, nor much grass either. Later, as I studied the Senate hearings on the park bill, with all the talk of "grazing rights," I thought of this incident. Much of this vast area can support no grazing at all. It is a soul-satisfying country, but cows can't live on scenery.

Two days later, having enjoyed our bird's-eye view, we re-entered the park area from another direction to explore the canyons at close quarters. "During the next hour or so," remarked our host at the wheel of his jeep, "we'll be going down about a hundred million years." The Superintendent of nearby Arches National Monument, he was one of the best "jeep herders" in Utah, which is to say one of the best this side of the moon—the imaginative pictures of whose surface might have been drawn from the country that now surrounded us. We were already below the buffy-red

Entrada sandstone which, with the softer mudstone beneath it, has made the spectacular forms which occur in Arches Monument; and we had passed through the Navajo formation below that. The rock walls here were Wingate sandstone, with vertical seams and streaks of blue-black "desert varnish"—an exudation of manganese oxide which gives the polished effect referred to by Powell in his journal. Here we

had our first good look at the Indian petroglyphs or rock carvings, whose exact origins are still shrouded in mystery. Beneath a slightly projecting ridge, which shielded it from the weather, was a rock wall the size of a barn door and equally flat. Virtually every square inch was covered with some design or picture: six-fingered hands and six-toed feet (why six?); lines of little men in silhouette, like a child's cut-out joined hand to hand; rams with curving horns; men with bows and arrows shooting deer; stretched hides; squiggly snake-like lines and circles and the tracks of a running rabbit. (Elsewhere we saw a fine petroglyph of a mammoth.) Many of the pictures stood out sharply, light buff against the dark background, as if they had been cut yesterday; others had been darkened by the slow deposition of desert varnish—a clue to their date if the rate of deposition can be determined.

Farther along we came to a cool moist cave beneath a great ledge of overhanging rock, like the opening of a giant clamshell. At the inmost recess, where the sloping roof came down to the dirt floor, lay a spring-fed pool, with maidenhair fern growing in the crevices above it, as it might have grown in a mist-filled mountain gorge. The contrast between the cave's microclimate and arid heat outside underscored the obvious fact, which we sometimes forget in the East, that water is life. As historians like Bernard DeVoto and Walter Prescott Webb have pointed out, the easterner's concept of land values and the schoolbook stereotype of "frontier independence" both collapse before the fact that landownership in the absence of water is meaningless. The Indians who once dwelt in these canyons were slowly driven elsewhere, not by warlike invaders from outside, but by unbearable years of drought. The cave where we now stood, with its precious spring, was clearly a focal point of Indian life, as it will be for tomorrow's tourists if the park is established.

On the same wall with the maidenhair fern were pictographs, not cut in the rock but painted in red pigment, recalling the similar Indian paintings of caribou and moose and other north-woods creatures that we had studied from our canoe in the border-lakes country seven hundred miles to the north. These fragile rock paintings of unknown antiquity also reminded us how vulnerable is this still virgin land to casual destruction by the machine age, how it cries aloud for protection while yet there is time. One of the witnesses before the Senate Committee had been camping nearby: "The cave we camped in had Indian writings on the wall, and among them were thirteen handprints in red clay. . . . we found a rock with three metates in the top— you know, where they ground their corn. And I could picture the Indian women sitting around gossiping and grinding their corn . . . When we returned to the area a year or so later, someone had had a caterpillar tractor in there and turned over the rock that had the metates and they were no longer visible. The cave we were in had had a fire right under the handprints on the wall, and they were well smoked out. I think that things like this shouldn't be allowed to happen. . . ."

Fortunately many of the Indian ruins—dwellings, storehouses for corn, ceremonial buildings—are on inaccessible ledges where they have remained largely undisturbed. As we continued down one of the canyons, we spotted several of the low redstone structures, with their neat rectangular openings, perched like swallows' nests high above us in the canyon wall. One was easy to reach, and I climbed up to explore it. The roof had long since fallen in, but the walls still stood. In the mud daubing between the stone blocks was a thumbprint that could have been made last week, the whorls sharp and clear enough to satisfy any detective who might be on that Indian's trail. But the trail would have led back to the age of Charlemagne.

The jeep track we were following now began to descend in earnest. Below the sheer cliffs were talus slopes of gray-purple and greenish shales. In geological terms, we were descending from the Lower Jurassic to the Upper Triassic period, back to the time before birds or mammals had appeared on earth. The reptiles, of course, had already been flourishing for millions of years. Elsewhere in Canyonlands, on the slopes above the Colorado River, near a wall covered with petroglyphs, I had seen fine specimens of dinosaur tracks. Just what, I wondered, did the Indians make of them?

The walls above us were becoming more strangely sculptured and involute at every turn, ranging in color from red-brown to maroon to a creamy white. We were in the so-called Cutler formation and on our vertical time scale were down to the Permian, over two hundred million years away. It would be hard to find a place that conveys such a dramatic sense of time: human time and geological time, two concepts so different from each other in scale that a single word is inadequate to cover both. The Indian petroglyph and the footprint of the dinosaur. A thousand years —forty or fifty generations—is at least conceivable in human terms. But a hundred million years makes no mental image at all; one has to accept it almost as an act of faith. Perhaps our minds cannot encompass such distances in time because our residence here has been so relatively short. *Homo sapiens* has evolved too recently even to make a respectable fossil. On that now familiar time scale projecting the history of the earth over a single year, he first appears during the last minutes before midnight on December 31. Bearing in mind the nearby uranium mines, any New Year's celebration seems premature.

This time scale is useful in considering the immediate question of a national park. It is an ominous fact that, in the long chain of evolution, the latest link, man, has suddenly acquired alchemic powers to alter whatever he touches. No species before man has been able to change more than a tiny fraction of his habitat. Now there is but a tiny fraction that he has left unchanged. A bulldozer undoes in an hour the work of a million years. The natural world becomes a thing to be manipulated. "You don't push nature around very easily," one of our leading young scientists is quoted as saying. Then he added eagerly, "But maybe we are getting to that point." The point of no return. If all outdoors is to be subdued to our immediate practical purposes, then the entire national park concept is nonsense; and to add a new park to the system is to compound our foolishness. For a national park might be defined as an area in which, by federal statute, nature may not be pushed around.

Desert camping has its own peculiar appeal to the amateur of nature. For one thing, the very sparseness of the natural scene gives him some hope of getting reasonably acquainted with it on a short visit. Some years ago my wife and I were dry-camping in a true desert, of a very different sort from Canyonlands: the Organ Pipe Cactus Monument in Arizona, close to the border of Mexico. Used to pitching our tent in wooded country where so much life goes on unseen, we could not help feeling that here in the desert everything was, so to speak, spread out on display. It would have taken a blind man not to see the incredibly bright yellow-and-black Scott's oriole picked out by the setting sun on a distant hillside or the zebra-like Gila woodpecker pecking at the trunk of a nearby saguaro. The cacti which made up the principal vegetation were spaced far apart as if in a garden and almost wore their own labels: the organ pipe (which the Monument was set up to preserve), the barrel cactus, the prickly pear, the staghorn and fuzzy-bear cholla

(beware its needle-like fuzz!), and, dominating all, the giant saguaro, a thick pole with stubby arms raised against the sky. The fresh green stems of the paloverde and the flame-red spikes of the desert candle shouted their identity; and when I was slow in recognizing ironwood, it introduced itself by taking a huge nick out of my axe.

So here in Canyonlands—which is semi-desert—we quickly became familiar with the principal plants composing the threads of green along the dry beds of the so-called creeks, whose scoured rocks and rippled sand provide the only access to much of the interior. Looking down from above, we had seen bands of blue-green bordering the Colorado River and creeping up the canyons; now we were among those feathery branches of the tamarisk or salt cedar, with its delicate pink and yellow blossoms—an immigrant from the Mediterranean. There were snowberries and squawberries, corn grass and thistles, the bright blossom of the scarlet gilia, and the white, petunia-like flower of the thorn apple. A hummingbird was darting from one flower to the other. The only large tree was that trademark of the West, the cottonwood, and it was rare enough; we lunched in the shade of one of the widely scattered groves, by a live creek: a sort of oasis with grass underfoot and tracks of mule deer in the spongy earth nearby. A small puddle was full of tadpoles and tiny frogs, whose life cycle must be a continuous crash program to take advantage of the water while it lasts.

When I said that everything in a desert seems on display, I was of course omitting the mammal and reptile population. Here even the small animals are nocturnal; it is not so much a matter of concealment as of avoiding the fierce dehydrating rays of the sun. We did flush a few rabbits and ground squirrels during the day; tiny lizards darted over the rocks and a larger collared lizard scuttled in front of the jeep before diving into its hole. Evidence of night life was written in the sand; not only tracks of a deer, but small round footprints, rather like those of a fox, though not so straight in line: the bobcat, as much at home in these canyons as he is in our New England woods.

In Canyonlands, however, it is not the plants and animals but the fantastic rock formations that bring one up gasping at every new outlook. To be sure, it is sometimes difficult to say whether the gasps come from the beauty of the scenery or the unnatural sensation of climbing up a cliff in a series of switchbacks so sharp that the jeep occasionally has to back up the next "switch" instead of making the turn, providing an incomparable view over the rear wheel down into nothing. Seat belts fastened, we braced our feet and held our breath as our mechanical steed pitched and rolled up a hard polished slope to which one would hesitate to put a real horse. On the downslope, another quick change of scene: a flat sunken valley, lined with vertical walls, called a "graben" and caused by slowly dissolving salts which leave a cavity beneath the rock floor. Then a long stretch of golden grassland—its healthy state paradoxically due to the fact that there is no water in the area and hence none of the overgrazing by livestock that has reduced other areas of Canyonlands to thin grass and tumbleweed. And finally at the edge of this park-like area we came to the great spires of red and caramel rock that we had studied from afar, rising from the flats as abruptly and improbably as Stonehenge from Salisbury Plain.

Back at the canyon bottom, a few hundred yards from a magnificent natural arch, we spread our bedrolls beneath a great rock ledge, which sloped outwards just far enough to keep off a light drizzle, and which conveniently concentrated a puddle of rain water nearby. Perhaps this natural cistern is one reason why the Indians had liked the spot. For we lay down to sleep between squared stones that still outline the foundations of four ancient structures. Overhead, black swifts swept back and forth against the fading sky; and now the bats began to emerge zigzagging from their caves in the rock. Our thoughts returned to the crucial issue of the park.

The controversy over Canyonlands is important because, as I said, it represents a conflict of principle. The

persons who take such a strong stand on one side or the other are thinking of the future, of the whole thorny question of land requirements for an exploding population. Everyone agrees that a national park is a Good Thing. But when it comes down to specifics, opinions differ. How big should it be to accomplish its purpose? Just what, in fact, *is* its purpose? How will it affect the local and the national economy? What, if any, "secondary uses"—such as mining, grazing, and hunting—should be permitted? These questions go to the root of national park policy.

In the case of Canyonlands, Secretary Udall originally proposed the taking of approximately one million acres, which would have included the entire erosion basin as a geological unit. The bill introduced by Senator Moss of Utah—and the identical bill introduced in the House by Congressmen King and Peterson—drastically reduced this area to 330,000 acres. (Grand Canyon National Park is 673,000 acres.) This is considered by many who know the country well to be inadequate. The Governor of Utah, on the other hand, opposed the bill on the grounds that it was too much; he preferred a sort of fragmented park consisting of relatively small areas surrounding the principal scenic marvels.

Hearings on the Moss bill were held in Washington and in Utah. Almost seven hundred pages of testimony were printed. They are not bedside reading, but they do provide a vivid if somewhat chaotic picture of the democratic process at work. Everyone has his day in court: senators and congressmen, Park Service officials, spokesmen for the leading conservation organizations; foresters, state and local politicians, professors, engineers, bankers, miners, cattlemen, motel owners, licensed guides. Prepared statements are supplemented (and frequently illuminated) by off-the-cuff remarks. From this plethora of words a pattern begins to emerge. Practically everyone is for the park in principle; to the surrounding communities it would bring millions of tourist dollars every year. But a park, if it means anything at all, means rigid control of land use, and that is where the trouble begins. But allowing controlled mining and grazing and hunting (under certain conditions) within the boundaries of the park, by recognizing the principle of so-called "multiple use," the Moss bill represents a compromise with basic national park principles. Conservationists and others concerned with the integrity of the park system consider this a dangerous precedent; they would strike out this provision in the bill. At the opposite pole, local mining interests claim that the provision is not strong enough; they point out that the Secretary of the Interior "may prescribe such general regulations for the control of these activities as he deems necessary to preserve the scenic, scientific, and recreation values of the area." They want no regulation—which, being interpreted, means no park, except in name. As Secretary Udall has pointed out, this is like trying to have your cake and eat it too. More specifically, it is like allowing the wedding cake to be pulled apart in search of the ring and the thimble—which probably are not there anyway.

What resources would in fact be "locked up" if all commercial exploitation were prohibited? The whole place has been prospected for uranium with negative results. In any case—to quote Senator Anderson's haunting metaphor—"We have got more uranium rolling out of our ears than we know what to do with." A study made by the University of Utah shows that there may be other mineral deposits, but none are known of commercial value. Almost the entire area is under oil and gas lease: ten dry holes have been drilled; the eleventh, on the edge of the proposed park, brought in a producing well and is being excluded from the park area. Grazing rights in this arid country are insignificant; annual fees from the entire 330,000 acres amount to only $2,700. The Moss bill allows grazing to continue for twenty-five years, though it must be obvious to anyone who has camped in Canyonlands that the cows and the tourists are going to use the same stamping ground; i.e., the few spots that have water.

Deer hunting is a more emotional subject. The Moss bill provides for "the controlled reduction of wildlife in such park by hunters licensed by the State of Utah and deputized as rangers by the Secretary." As I said earlier, of all the pressures on the Park Service, the one for public hunting seems to arouse the loudest view halloo. When the Service uses its own personnel, as it has done in Yellowstone, scientifically to reduce the elk herds, there are cries of outrage from those who see wasted chances for sport. When specially licensed hunters are allowed to try their trigger fingers at it, as they were in Teton Park in Wyoming, the naturalists and conservationists cry havoc. The Chief Naturalist at Yellowstone supports their fears with statistics. Supposing that the reduction of the Yellowstone elk herd had been put in the hands of private hunters: "If their ability was equal to that of the 1,002 hunters in Grand Teton, nearly 18,000 hunters would have killed the 5,000 elk, plus 196 illegal moose, 410 illegal elk and seventeen men, along with an undetermined number of bears, coyotes, bighorn sheep, antelope, bison, mule deer and horses." In Canyonlands the issue is more one of principle than of powder and shot; comparatively few deer are taken within its boundaries. The chances of bagging illegal animals, including men, are even more remote. But to legalize park hunting by statute may be a precedent more dangerous than bullets.

Mining, grazing, hunting—each has its staunch adherents, yet all are fundamentally incompatible with the basic park concept. The term "multiple use" has become a sort of shibboleth. In the case of our national parks it is seriously misleading. In the first place, the proper use of our parks is itself multiple: wilderness preservation, recreation, protection of watersheds, sanctuaries for wildlife, undisturbed areas for scientific study. In the second place, commercial and recreational use are often mutually exclusive. For activities that disturb or deplete the land, the term "nonconforming use" is more accurate. In other words, a temporary exception rather than a permanent policy.

The battle will be fought to a finish on the floor of Congress. The traditional conflict between federal and states' rights will be renewed: state fish and game commissioners have gone on record urging Congress (in clear contradiction to existing policy) to leave management in their hands "whenever any authority is granted to the National Park Service to create any new areas or to increase the size of existing areas." The Utah commissioner, at the Canyonlands hearings, attacked "the autocratic and high-handed attitudes of the National Park Service" which threatened "the sovereignty of the State."

None of this, of course, is new, but it does make the Canyonlands issue worth studying. For as the developing embryo of an individual organism suggests earlier stages in the evolution of the species, so the study of a single park in embryo reminds us of the evolutionary history of the park system itself. The issues raised in the discussion of Canyonlands echo those raised when the first national park, Yellowstone, was established in 1872, when the Grand Canyon was saved by Teddy Roosevelt (its rim was once staked with mining claims), when the unique rain forest in Washington's Olympic Park was preserved from the axe, when Jackson Hole in the Tetons was added to the park system against local opposition to become one of Wyoming's greatest assets. They will be raised again whenever other parks are proposed. For the story of the national park concept is the story of the evolution of an idea, momentarily spotlighted in those glowing red-rock canyons at the heart of the Plateau Province.

CHAPTER 10

The Pressure on Our Parks

AN OCCASIONAL camping trip such as I have been describing here is no basis for grand generalizations about the entire park system. The Sunday visitor to the Metropolitan Museum of Art, however he may love some corners of it, is not thereby prepared to generalize on the purposes and management of art museums. Yet there is one impression I carry back from every trip: from the Alpine meadows of the Olympics, from the hot sands of the Virgin Is-

((153

lands, from the Appalachian Trail on the crest of the Smokies, or from the high tundra of Mount McKinley Park. It is simple wonder—and gratitude—that such places still exist; that such experience is still possible. This hasn't come about by chance. The very concept of a "national park" was revolutionary a hundred years ago. In Europe, parks were royal preserves, for the sport of a tiny minority. The idea of parks for all the people was of American origin. It is profoundly democratic. And it has worked so well that it now threatens to work its own destruction.

Taken all together, the national parks cover less than two per cent of the continental United States. The annual number of visitors amounts to about one third of our population. More leisure, more cars, more interest perhaps in outdoor nature. Theoretically this is fine. Actually it can be catastrophic. Those of us who avoid the most populated spots during the peak loads never see the worst of it, but the fact of overcrowding is everywhere evident. So, alas, is the prescription that may kill the patient: overdevelopment.

There is, of course, an inherent paradox in multitudes seeking wilderness solitude. Fortunately the millions who visit the parks do not have identical objectives. There are some people whose spiritual metabolism requires an occasional dose of what Thoreau called "the tonic of wildness." They are generally willing to work for what they get. Others go for fishing, for climbing, for photography, for nature study. Still others use the parks to give the whole family a week's inexpensive holiday in beautiful, healthy surroundings; they are probably happiest in a campground with close but congenial neighbors (I find that most people you meet at a park campground *are* congenial) where they find other children for theirs to play with. All these concerns are equally legitimate. Unhappily, there is also a very different type of visitor: the type that comes looking for ready-made entertainment. He thinks of a national park as a sort of drive-in bear garden. He stops his car among the redwoods, rolls the window down for a closer look, and complains: "Yeah, I see 'em, but what do you *do* here?"—as if he expected the forest to put on a floor show. He will never find what he wants in the parks while they remain parks. But what of the others?

The need to accommodate the crowds has inevitably led to compromise in preservation of the natural landscape. Let's face it: this hurts. Take for example the Great Smokies Park. As I said, we have returned there again and again, over a period of some twenty years. At one time Cades Cove was a favorite spot. You reached it by a narrow twisting road over the mountain; the campground was a level area beside the river with three or four picnic tables and a privy. Today a wide graded road comes down the valley and there is a city of tents with all modern conveniences and firewood for sale. Something has been lost, but an awful lot of people are being made—or rather are making themselves—happy. I like to think that their children are learning to love the outdoors and unconsciously preparing themselves to defend it.

Some "development" is necessary; the obvious danger today is that, under pressure, it may be going hog-wild. I venture to suggest that much of this activity—particularly the building of roads for fast cars and "marinas" for fast boats—is based on a mistaken premise. It is assumed that the public (as distinguished from the automobile and motor-boat industries) demands these things, and that the parks cannot be "used" without them. Is this true?

Let us go back a moment to the initial problem: too little room for too many people. The space available in the national parks is not big enough for all who want to use them. But the size of a park is directly related to the manner in which you use it. If you are in a canoe traveling at three miles an hour, the lake on which you are paddling is ten times as long and ten times as broad as it is to the man in a speedboat going thirty. An hour's paddle will take you as far away as an hour in a speedboat—if there are no speedboats. In other words, more people can use the same space with the same results. Whenever we return from a canoe trip, someone is sure to ask us how many miles we traveled. We never know; and we couldn't care less. I do know, however, that every road that replaces a footpath, every outboard motor that replaces a canoe paddle, shrinks the area of the park. And don't let anyone tell you that this attitude means discrimination in favor of the young and athletic. The man who is too feeble to paddle a canoe should never go tearing off in an outboard motorboat; after all, he may have to paddle home. Highways, of course, can shrink parks faster than anything else; from my limited experience I think that they represent the greatest "clear and present danger" to the park system. Walking for three consecutive days along the Appalachian Trail in the Great Smokies, through dark forests of virgin red spruce and sunny "balds" flaming with azalea, I have shuddered to recall that a "scenic" highway was once planned for the whole length of this trail. (In addition to the adequate highway across Newfound Gap and up to Clingman's Dome.) Camping on the ocean strip of Olympic Park, I was acutely aware that only the heroic efforts of men like Olaus J. Murie and William O. Douglas and other devoted conservationists have kept this wild beach from degenerating into the shoulders of another speedway. Road development could be fatal to Isle Royale or the Virgin Islands Park. Both islands are blessed with the absence of automobiles. On Isle Royale there is only a foot trail, and on St. John a rocky jeep road runs along the spine. Both islands would be spoiled if a highway were ever built.

Obviously, some roads are essential to the enjoyment of the parks. The test is, will a road destroy the very thing—the basic value—it is supposed to give access to? In wartime parlance: "Is this trip necessary" at fifty miles an hour? One thinks of the Chinese philosopher who will spend an entire day on a hillside, listening to the ripple of a brook, contemplating the shifting light on a distant mountain peak, and studying the profile of the wind-blown pine above his head. He has not covered much distance, but he may have traveled far.

Since our parks are not used principally by Chinese philosophers, there is bound to be a demand for "improvements"; but they can be carried to excess. A trained observer described a new high-speed road being built through a park where it seemed quite unnecessary: "While the former road wound pleasantly through the spruce and fir forests, and ambled across open parks, the new pushes ruthlessly over all obstructions, seeming to say: 'Stand back, Nature—you're in the way. Here comes progress!'" One can only hope for restraint, in both central planning and local execution. To paraphrase the poet, unless we use the snaffle and the curb all right there won't *be* any bloody horse. This is not a military operation; we don't have to build the Burma Road before frost or even to get our trenches dug before dawn. We are not at war with the wilderness.

· · ·

((157

In our travels my wife and I have come to recognize among the park personnel—perhaps especially among the men in the naturalist branch—a sense of mission to educate the public to the true uses of their parks. By contagious enthusiasm rather than by preaching, the men in the field are

making the visitor aware of the values (including the spiritual values) he should expect to find in a park. These men have a dedication to their job; in fact, nothing less could attract and hold the class of person whom one finds everywhere in the Service. Join a "nature walk" in the Olympic rain forest or among the Alpine flowers: likely as not it will be led by a young ranger-naturalist who is raising a family on a tiny budget while he works for a Ph.D. in botany, not in anticipation of an academic career, but to serve in the parks. Talk to the older men: you will find experienced scientists whom any university would be glad to hire, men who have made original contributions in every branch of natural history, ecologists following in the footsteps of Aldo Leopold, botanists whom Bartram and Michaux would have enjoyed as fellow explorers. Show the slightest interest in what they are doing and they will respond far beyond the call of duty. They know that the ultimate answer to the problem of the parks is not so much in physical development as in education. Here is where the Division of Interpretation—with branches in natural history, history, archaeology, museums, and information—plays such an important role. The coming generation will decide the fate of the parks; hence the need to extend these services beyond the parks themselves into the schools—a mission for broadening minds, not roads.

If there is a keystone in the whole complex structure, it is, I believe, the concept of the wilderness area, the object of which is to preserve for present and future generations some part of our country in its original state, unaltered by man. The scientific and cultural value of such areas is immeasurable; they are to our national park and forest system what its libraries, laboratories, and museums are to a great university. The establishment of wilderness areas is of course much more recent than the founding of the park system itself. Scarcely more than twenty years ago a number of farsighted conservationists managed to get legal recognition of the value of wilderness and the necessity to act before it is too late. Here there can be no compromise. You cannot "selectively cut" a rain forest and still have a rain forest; you cannot bring a gasoline engine, on wheels or afloat, into a wilderness and still have a wilderness.

In an era of exploding population, if we are to preserve the parks without enforcing quotas on visitors, the park system itself must be enlarged: to provide more space for more people, to preserve the finest natural features of our landscape from commercial development, to protect areas of historic significance. For example, the recently established Cape Cod National Seashore will accomplish, to a limited extent, all three objectives. Though its area is not great, it is a still unspoiled bit of the Atlantic seashore rich in history, in folklore, in bird life, in spectacular natural beauty. "A first glimpse of the great outer beach of Cape Cod," writes Henry Beston in an introduction to Thoreau's classic, "is one of the most memorable experiences in all America." At the other extreme, the desert country of Canyonlands offers a chance to preserve great areas of open space, scenic grandeur, and remains of ancient civilizations. In addition to new parks such as this, we desperately need more room, *outside* the existing park system, to relieve the pressure on that tiny percentage of our national heritage which we are morally obligated to preserve in its primeval state. Cannot Congress establish a system of supplementary park areas under some different designation (preferably adjacent to the national parks themselves) which will be specifically intended for camping and outdoor recreation: in which ski tows and motorboats and other activities and social amusements will be permitted, where there will be adequate accommodations for large numbers of people amid attractive surroundings? The land already exists within our national forests, and surely the problems of its administration, whether by the Park Service or the Forest Service, are not insuperable.

But I am straying into the realm of high-level administration. One thing I do know from personal experience: there are innumerable opportunities for outdoor adventure, from an hour's walk in a Town Forest to a week's backpacking trip on a mountain trail, which do not involve the use of the national parks at all. One way to relieve crowding in the parks is to develop these local alternatives. Take our waterways, for example. My wife and I once paddled and sailed a canoe for a hundred and fifty miles down Lake Champlain and the Richelieu River without, as I recall it, meeting a single other canoe. Many rivers throughout the country provide quick escape from the mechanized world, but infinitely more would do so if they were redeemed from their present uses as dumps and open sewers. We hear much today about "urban renewal." A program of "rural renewal," and an accelerated program of open space acquisition near our centers of population, would provide closer to home many of the values that people now feel can be found only in the national parks. Like a work of art, the natural scene is something that can be "used" without being used up. How we use it in America will have a very real bearing on the sort of people we become.

When I think of the parks I recall a scene one July evening on Hurricane Ridge, which overlooks the whole vast range of the Olympics. For several nights we had had the campground to ourselves: a meadow at snowline, on the edge of the glacier lilies. We were slightly disappointed when a large family group settled in opposite us; the peace would be destroyed, the spell would be broken. We were wrong. They had come to enjoy the wilderness, not to dispel it. Their quiet voices didn't reach across the grassy space between us. The black-tailed deer that grazed every morning and evening within steps of our tent were not disturbed. While we were cooking supper we looked up to see the whole group standing quite motionless, like a tableau in the setting sun, around the ribbon of blue smoke from their campfire. They were saying grace.

CHAPTER 11

The Uses of a Canoe

P<small>ADDLE</small> your own canoe" is a misleading expression. A canoe is a boat for two. It is infinitely adaptable. You can paddle it, pole it, or sail it. You can sleep in it or under it. You can transport it in a baggage car, on a trailer, on top of your automobile or your back. It will float on a heavy dew, yet it is not too frail for the open ocean. In rapids it will give you the thrill of a ski run; on a lake at evening it is the embodiment of peace. A canoe, like rum, is a ready mixer.

It goes well with fishing or birding or camping or loafing; even—if you are seeking a Permanent Bow Paddle—with courting.

Long before our expeditions to the border lakes and Algonquin Park my wife and I had learned the joys of canoe trips nearer home from a second-hand sixteen-footer, picked up at bargain rates from a canoe livery on the Concord River. We rigged a lateen sail of spinnaker cloth (nine by nine by eight feet along the leech), with spars of one-inch doweling, and a mast from a closet pole, stepped forward of the bow seat in a large curtain-rod socket. This outfit was christened on Lake Champlain, during a trip that began as an afternoon sail and developed into a five-day run down the length of the lake and well into Canada. In a canoe too many plans are as bad as too many gadgets: at the very most, plan the grand strategy and leave the tactics to the water and the weather. Over canoeists there watches a special Providence that takes the place of logical thought. Witness what happened to us one June morning on the upper Connecticut River. Here, near the Canadian border, the mighty Connecticut is only a fair-sized trout stream; but there had been a week of rain and the brown water was swirling high along the banks. Fishing was over for the time being. Even the perseverant couple from Boston, with whom we had fished the previous day, must be discouraged by now. But conditions, poor for taking trout, were good for a quick-water canoe run. We set out, our vague destination a town some twenty-five miles downstream. For ten or twelve miles all went well. Then a long stretch of heavy rapids or "haystacks" appeared ahead; another moment and they were lapping over the gunwale. We did not upset. We submerged slowly, gracefully, like a submarine when no pursuer is in sight. Then we bounced on the bottom, grace departed, and we slithered ashore. And here is the point: on the bank, as if awaiting our arrival and submersion, stood the couple from Boston, with sweaters to warm us outside, rum to warm us inside, and a car to take us back to camp. From twenty-five miles of river, they had chosen this one spot to cast a fly. At least they didn't come home empty-handed.

Quick-water canoeing in the rapids is a sport of the early spring, when every brook brings melted snow down from the mountains and rivers run high. Involving both paddle and pole, it is a fine and strenuous art. From brief experience in and under white water, I can only suggest that an old keel-less canoe, ripe for smashing, is the beginner's best equipment. The absence of a keel makes the bottom more vulnerable but the boat itself easier to worm between the rocks. On a quick-water run, your dignity should also be ripe for smashing. You may find yourself lifted out of the boat like a monkey on your pole or sitting alone in midstream clinging to a boulder by your coccyx. The man on the river in April need yield nothing to the skier on the snow slopes above him.

Swift or smooth, broad as the Hudson or narrow enough to scrape your gunwales, every river is a world of its own, unique in pattern and personality. Each mile on a river will take you further from home than a hundred miles on a road. You will see more in an hour than a motorist will see in a week. Birds, for example. River valleys are the songbirds' paradise. In New England, the Hudson and Connecticut valleys are flyways of migration, and small streams generally provide food and cover along their banks, as well as the water that all birds must have. It is amusing to paddle down some quiet river, screened from the surrounding country by dense alder thickets, and try to determine by means of bird songs alone the nature of the land through which you are passing. Meadowlarks and bobolinks indicate fields and pastures; robins and bluebirds and orioles also mean open country—orchards perhaps, or scattered trees; but if you hear the soft voice of the thrushes, or the "teacher! TEACHER! TEACHER!" of the ovenbird, you are probably in the deep woods.

The spotted sandpiper and the kingfisher are characteristic birds of the New England rivers, but the bird I associated most of all with canoeing is the American merganser or sheldrake. On one trip down the Connecticut, we drove before us no less than four families of sheldrakes —the gray, rufous-headed mother ducks flopping noisily ahead to attract our attention, while the ducklings alternately hid in the bushes along the shore and sped like little aquaplanes after their parents. It seemed as if they would wear themselves out. Several times we hid the boat and tried to drive them back upstream, but in vain.

Birds add flavor to any outdoor activity; even the disappointment of losing a large trout is tempered by finding the nest of a waterthrush at the edge of the pool. Yet the haunts and habits of birds are no more entertaining than the haunts and habits of bird-lovers. We will choose incredible places in which to pursue our hobby. Sometimes the choice is involuntary. Caught once by a thunder squall on a big lake, my wife and I had raced for a cottage on the nearest point. It was locked. Out back, however, stood a bright virgin one-holer. A squeeze, but rainproof—what is more, a perfect blind for bird study. Through the new moon in the door we could watch sandpipers and killdeers running over

the beach, ducks feeding off shore, and in the marsh grass a
statuesque great blue heron and a bittern or bog-pumper.
(The bittern, by the way, has shown that the habits of
bird-lovers can be as odd as their haunts. On one occasion
an important bird book was almost abandoned at the moment of publication because the editors could not agree as
to whether the bittern while "pumping" said *ugh* PLUM
pud'n or *ugh plum* PUD'N.)

A canoe with a sail is like a horse with wings. It doesn't
come natural. But there is a place for Pegasus if you give
him room to cavort in. To sail a canoe with any freedom,
you need a broad river or, better still, a lake or salt-water
harbor. Here, with leeboards and a light load, you can even

beat to windward. For exploring salt marshes and tidal estuaries, as well as for lake and river travel, a canoe has the edge on an outboard motorboat; you may see a duck before it takes flight, hear the yellowlegs answer your whistle, smell the rich mud of the marsh. A canoe trip at sea is something of a tour de force, though one can take long voyages in good summer weather. Here your horse wants wings. On a broad expanse of water, you may paddle till your back aches but you only inch along. Hour after hour, distant headlands remain distant; there is little change of scene—whereas a river has something new for you around every bend, and a chain of lakes a new scene at the end of every portage. Yet salt-water paddling may also have its moments of perverse satisfaction, such as the time we smugly threaded our way into Marblehead Harbor through the cream of America's racing yachts, helplessly becalmed outside.

But to me a canoe under sail will always mean Lake Champlain. That first trip down the hundred-mile lake and a stretch of the Richelieu River gave a taste of everything: sailing, paddling, excitement, and peace. Heading north, we had sailed through the narrows at Ticonderoga and Crown Point. Behind us lay a stretch of lake that had seemed more like a sluggish river, with pickerelweed lining the banks, and red-winged blackbirds rising from the cattails. Only the bantam lighthouses had given promise of wider waters to come. Now the promise was being fulfilled. Champlain was no longer a river. Far to the west lay the gray folds of the Adirondacks; to the east, half hidden from our sight by the sail, rose the knobbier mountains of Vermont. My wife lay back to the mast, the sheet wrapped round her foot. I leaned on the steering paddle as it curved with the weight of water. Probably we were not making more than five or six miles an hour. But speed is relative, and with the rail a few inches above the white-capped surface we were flying. Two days of this and we had reached Valcour Island—the scene of Benedict Arnold's famous naval battle with Burgoyne. Approaching the hogback island after our long sail, we looked in vain for a camping

spot on its steep slopes. A tiny ledge of gravel at length appeared. Here was room for a bed and a fire. We landed gently and lifted the canoe out of the water, built a small fire of driftwood, and blew up the air mattresses. As we finished our supper the wind dropped. A waxing moon dimmed the last embers of the fire. The gulls ceased to cry. Back and forth between two headlands, forming the cusps of a crescent beach, flew dozens of bats. The pebbles of the beach itself gave forth a low rumble, quite unlike the hiss of waves on sand, but equally good for sleep.

It was on this same trip that our canoe became a ship. In four days of sailing, we had reached the northern end of Lake Champlain and were crossing the line into Canada. A canoe, I expected, would be beneath official notice. On the contrary, a customs officer examined us as thoroughly as he would a seagoing vessel, plumbed our hold and recorded our duffel with meticulous care. Satisfied at last, he gave me a certificate declaring that "the Master of the *S.S. Paul Brooks*" had complied with all regulations. Sixteen feet of sturdy ship, swollen with new dignity, headed down the Richelieu River.

The canoeists' Providence that had hauled us out of the Connecticut River made another fine last gesture as we left Lake Champlain. In shirts and shorts we were sitting among the well-dressed passengers on the Montreal–New York train, with the boat in the baggage car, our destination Whitehall at the head of the lake. From the window we watched our trip unfold, like a motion-picture film speeding in reverse. (I figured two days' canoeing, on the average, for each hour of a fast train.) Our automobile was still parked by the lake—and the railroad—some miles above Whitehall. How to return to it was a problem yet unsolved. We saw it flash by the window. But express trains do not stop for canoeists. And then, incredibly, the train slowed down and stopped. The northbound was going by. To the consternation of the other passengers, we leaped from our seats, slipped out the door, and walked back along the tracks. . . .

America has turned her back upon her rivers. Once her life blood, they are now too often her drains; the path to the front door has become the back-yard dump. Fishermen have already done much to change this; perhaps canoeists will do the rest. Here, as I have suggested earlier, lies a great opportunity for recreation near home, thus relieving the pressures on our highways and our parks. Outboard motors are not the answer: there is no sense in cleaning up our rivers only to pollute them again with the stink and roar of the gasoline engine. As population growth continues to encroach on the few quiet spots within range of our daily lives, the canoe looks better and better; a good neighbor and traveling companion that does not destroy the wonder of the outdoors but leaves it intact for the next man.

CHAPTER 12

Between the Tides

THE surf has many voices, but to hear them you
must literally keep your ear to the ground. My wife and
I learned this the hard way when our worn air mattresses
breathed their last as we lay in our tent on Sanibel Island
off the west coast of Florida. Sanibel is not a park, but
it has a national wildlife refuge at its center and many
miles of unspoiled shell beach on its outer margins, as
seductive in their way as the shimmering sands of St. John.

It was early spring, and we were camped in a grove of
feathery Australian pines at the edge of the beach, a few
yards above high-tide line. Having fallen asleep to the

regular but infinitely varied cadence of breaking waves, I awoke to a new sound: a rising wind, I thought, soughing in the pines overhead; a storm brewing, and time to check the tent ropes. Yet no sooner had I raised my head than the mysterious sighing ceased. It was not in the air at all but in the ground—sea against shell. A New Englander, I had failed to recognize surf with a southern accent. This was different from the boom of breakers on Maine granite, from the "grating roar of pebbles" that Matthew Arnold heard on Dover Beach and could equally well have heard north of Boston, even from the hiss of wavelets sinking into the summer sands of Cape Cod. To me a beach of crushed shell and shell sand was something strange, and its voice had the impact of any first awareness.

A tent at the water's edge may lack the amenities—and in a storm the security—of a proper bedroom, but it has its own delights. We were not (to use an emetic phrase) "roughing it." A scant quarter-mile from the nearest inn, we simply preferred a detached room with housekeeping facilities. Living out of doors, one is more a part of the day and of the night. The rising moon, just past the full, is a disk of brightness on our light cotton ceiling. Orion's Belt is framed by the peak of our three-cornered door. The slightest shifts of wind are betrayed by the billowing of our walls, now on the one side, now on the other. The scent of wet pine needles is mingled with the salt tang of the open ocean and the subtle odor of decaying seaweed and debris from the deep.

Not even the hard ground, which leapt up to take the place of our dead air mattresses—with a special affinity for hips and shoulder blades—could keep us long from sleep. The cry of shore birds awoke us at last, and none too soon.

Sunrise had reached its climax; the sky in the triangle was a mottled mass of delicate pinks and grays. We watched the footlights fade and the house lights go up; then, with a quick look right and left for early shell collectors, ran into the gentle surf. This was no character-building North Shore dip, where gooseflesh goes with godliness, but a luxurious South Sea wallow. So began our first day on the island. We decided to spend it introducing ourselves to the oldest residents in their respective haunts: the mollusks on the beach and mud flats, the palms and cacti and tropical flora of the mainland, the rich bird life of the marsh and mangroves. Breakfast we cooked at the water's edge, partially frustrating the mosquitoes who swarmed around our camp site in the pines. I soon learned that a shell beach—if you have the right wife—makes a good kitchen. There is plenty of small driftwood for fuel and you don't have to build a fireplace. You dig one; and so long as the packed sand and shell remains moist it will support your grate without collapsing. While we ate our bacon and eggs, we identified our alarm clock: a flock of twenty willets. Tall, straight-billed waders, when at rest they appeared dull gray and wooden; but when they took flight with sharp cries they displayed a magnificent pattern of jet black and white. Behind the willets, not venturing so far into the water, was our clock's "soft" alarm: a dozen black-bellied plovers, with their sad three-note whistle. Out in deep water, a cormorant perched motionless on an old channel marker.

While we were watching these neighbors, there arrived on unhurried wings that most sedately beautiful of birds, the snowy egret. He alighted nearby, and immediately the whole scene seemed to sharpen into focus. At close range he was a Japanese ink painting come to life: the pure white

plumage with drooping crest, the bold black brush strokes of the bill and legs. And if a snowy egret is a work of art, the dramatic rescue of his species from extinction has made him also a symbol: a symbol of a relatively new attitude toward the natural world, in which other living creatures are something more than mere commodities for the use of man.

Our egret, as we soon found ourselves calling him, had his own strip of beach which he patrolled, to the east and west of our tent, wading with slow, fastidious steps as he fished the shallows, occasionally darting his dagger-like beak beneath the waves. Apparently this was his territory. He shared it unconcernedly with the willets and the plovers and the little "peeps," but during the week we lived on the beach we saw no trespassing by his peers.

The late March sun was already hot when we had done up the breakfast dishes, buried the fire, and set out down the beach. A long, scythe-shaped strip of sand, it ranged in color from dazzling white where it backed up against the pines to a warm gray where the scythe blade met the sea. Close up, one saw that the grade was not uniform to the water's edge. A ridge of shells and shell fragments marked high-tide line, in cross section a tiny moraine, gently sloping to the landward side, dropping off sharply seaward. Shells everywhere, and on the edge of the ebbing tide an occasional live mollusk, half buried in the sand. My wife and I, conchological ignoramuses, felt like tyro birdwatchers suddenly set down in the middle of the spring warbler migration. We were in a shell collector's heaven, without as yet being able to tell the cherubim from the seraphim, or the rose cockles from the bloody clams. (A name, this, not an epithet.) Surprisingly quickly, thanks to the *Field Guide to the Shells* and other shell books, the mass sorted itself out, the eye skipping over identified species and resting on the unfamiliar, just as the trained ear will pick out a strange bird song from the confusing spring chorus. The more we dug and sorted and waded watchfully in the shallows, the more we became fascinated by the forms and colors and textures in the world of mollusks. They ranged from huge, barnacle-encrusted horse conchs, several pounds in weight, to tiny bright cochinas, the size of a child's fingernail. (And we found baby horse conchs too that you could put in a timble.) Scallops in irresistible combinations of red and gray and ocher, rough to the touch, each seeming a shade more lovely than the last one you picked up; glassy-smooth "olives"; sturdy fighting conchs and delicate moon shells; thick cockles, brown or rose or yellow within; translucent "paper figs" and pure-white angel wings and pencil-like horn shells and augers. The names were almost as attractive as the creatures themselves: cat's paw, sailor's ear, old maid's curl, jewel box, alphabet cone. The best hunting, we found, was at dead low tide on a shelf about knee-deep in the water. Between waves there was a tantalizing moment when the ledge was almost exposed. In this split second we tried to sort out the rich display and pounce on some new treasure, before the next wave blotted out the picture. Here we found the live creatures, often feeding on one another (hardly a horse conch that was not attached to some other mollusk it was devouring), and here they were most exquisite, the pigments in their shells unfaded by exposure to the sun.

As the tide flowed back and we sat down to eat our lunch and sort our treasures, we were reminded of the close kinship between the forms and patterns of nature and

((177

the art of man. For nowhere is it more apparent than in the shapes and colors of shells. I recalled seeing in Boston's Museum of Science a conch shell that had been sawed through lengthwise to show the inner spiral; beside it, almost its twin, was a photograph of the famous staircase at Blois. So with the banded tulip shells in my hand. Their inner form and outer decoration had the rhythms—the repetition with variations—of a Persian fabric or an Attic frieze. They seemed to say that nature and art are identical in their ultimate aim: the creation of cosmos out of chaos. And why not? The story of evolution is the story of each form of life exploiting as best it can the situation it finds itself in; relating itself to the whole; using the available material; making sense, so to speak, out of its predicament. And, of course, creating new material and a new situation in the process. Is the concern of the artist very different?

Today my wife and I had our own simpler predicament: not that of the artist, but of the donkey of the fable faced with the choice between equally enticing bales of hay. The beach was beguiling. So was the interior of the island; indeed it was even more exotic to northern eyes. Less than a hundred yards back from the shore we found a sort of miniature desert of porous shell sand, with prickly pear and other cacti bursting out in improbable red and waxy yellow flowers. Tropical zebra butterflies, bright yellow bands on jet black, fluttered feebly in the shelter of the mangroves. Coon tracks led from the scrub out to the beach; not only shell collectors were interested in the cargo from the last high tide. Farther inland we came to broad savannahs dotted with coconut palms. Scores of turkey

vultures—with an occasional black vulture—circled overhead. A water turkey sailed by, its snake-like head thrust
forward in flight. On the edge of a bulky nest at the top of a
dead pine stood two young ospreys ready for flight: here,
in March, at the same stage of growth as the two I had seen
and sketched in Ontario in early August. Finally we came
to the fresh-water marsh and the federal wildlife refuge that
was our last destination of the day.

"I moments live, who lived but years. . . ." Henry
Thoreau knew more of these moments than most of us,
since he insisted on a broad margin to his life. Yet during
even the quietest day outdoors there is often a sort of peak
of awareness, a moment when something extra is given, for
which one instinctively returns thanks. For us it came just
before sunset as we stood in the lookout of the refuge,
twelve feet above the marsh and maybe twelve inches above
the ravenous mosquitoes. Coot were muttering in the maze
of waterways below us, a pair of boat-tailed grackles were
noisily nest-building in an adjacent hummock; a red-bellied
woodpecker, chased away by a flicker from his favorite
coconut palm, had taken refuge briefly a yard from our
heads. As if to prevent the familiar prairie warbler's song
from making us feel too much at home, an alligator slithered
across the path into the water, till only the two knobs of
his eyes showed where he lay. Silently, flying so low that
we had missed his approach, a great black-winged bird
swept by, creasing the water with his down-pointed beak:
the black skimmer, long familiar to us as the hero of Rachel
Carson's *Under the Sea-Wind*. Then, as if this were not
enough for one day, the great show began. In a sky still blue
to the eastward but washed with crimson in the west, there
appeared on the northern horizon an irregular group of tiny

dots. They grew, took shape; the dots became white, the slow wingbeats discernible. These were not egrets: in the binoculars we could distinguish outstretched necks, down-curved bills. White ibis! In another moment the dense, dark clump of mangrove trees which rose above the marsh had blossomed like a huge flowering shrub as the ibises dropped down among the swaying branches, flapping once or twice to get their balance before settling in for the night. Flock followed flock as the birds came in to roost from their distant feeding grounds. Now they were being joined by herons—Louisiana, little blue, American and snowy egrets —arriving in small groups or singly rather than in large flocks. We quickly learned to tell the white herons from the ibises by the way they came in for a landing: the former gliding down smoothly, the latter "stalling" just above the treetops, side-slipping and tumbling down into the branches. Still they kept coming, till it seemed that the trees could hold no more. (We supposed that somewhere in the melee was our egret; at dawn he would be back with us on the beach.) Finally as the color faded from the sky the great roost came to rest. With a sense of fulfillment we set out for our own roost in the pines by the shore.

The thing about sleeping outdoors, as I said, is that you feel a part of the night. But I'd rather be a part of some nights than of others—and this was obviously going to be one of the others. By the time we had groped our way through the dusk to our tent a strong onshore wind was tugging at the guy ropes, which we had fortunately an- chored to trees, since pegs won't hold in sandy soil. A few hours later (no signs of Orion tonight) we were wondering whether anything was going to hold; in fact, whether this was really a tent or a misplaced balloon jib. We secured the sidewalls to two long logs, piled anything heavy we could find against the windward opening, and tried to forget what we had heard about equinoctial storms. Actually the wind probably never reached what the Beaufort Scale pictur- esquely calls a "whole gale"; in the downpour that followed we were happy that the tent had held. Morning revealed a heavy surf and a beach whose whole complexion had changed during the night: the ridges of shell flattened, the orange peels that we had carefully buried scattered messily

around with the churned-up sand. Nevertheless we saw no reason why breakfast could not be cooked in this newly decorated kitchen. Digging a deep hole for the fire and piling sand for a windbreak, we got coffee water boiling and eggs frying in the pan. Just as they were ready to serve we looked behind us. The concept of the big "ninth wave" may be just folklore, but something of the sort was upon us, whatever its serial number. Before you could say "The Sea Around Us," fire, coffee, and eggs had returned to the Mother from whom we all sprang.

Our flock of willets flew up in momentary alarm and then, as the great wave receded, calmly continued hunting their breakfast. I suppose that it was unscientific to detect a note of derision in their shrill cry.

CHAPTER 1 3

Mexico's California

I т і s said that the Spanish missionaries to Baja (Lower) California—then known simply as "California"—occasionally ran into trouble when preaching eternal damnation during spells of cold weather. The shivering Indians in their roofless huts all demanded to go to hell. Three centuries later, when almost our entire continent has been tamed and put to use, this austere and empty peninsula, stretching southward from the Mexican border to the Tropic of Cancer, seems like a bit of heaven at any time of year. Particularly so if you have a chance to explore it, as my wife and I did one April, in the company of a group of distinguished naturalists under the aegis of the Belvedere Scientific Fund. Our journey had a long-range purpose. If the scenic and scientific values of this unique peninsula were better understood—the quiet deep-blue bays, the strange cactus "forests," and above all the island homes of the rare sea birds—might not a bit of it be saved from exploitation while yet there is time?

Baja is not a country that throws itself at you, flaunting its charms. If you like to take your scenery from the highway, in low-slung, knee-actioned ease, avoid Baja at all costs—including the cost of a broken axle. By modern standards it is a roadless area, though paradoxically containing the oldest road in North America: El Camino Real, the King's Highway, built by the Spanish padres to connect their chain of missions from La Paz near the tip of the peninsula twelve hundred miles northward to San Francisco. Some of its ancient villages can be reached by air, in planes that don't need a runway. The interior is best explored by jeep or—for long journeys—by specially equipped truck. On a ten days' trip we could at least sample bits of an ever various desert, by truck and on foot; poke about virgin bays in small boats and visit some of the offshore islands where sea birds still nest in fabulous abundance, yet where the survival of at least one species is already threatened by man.

It was a clear morning when we headed south from Tucson, Arizona, in an eight-passenger plane, for our rendezvous on Concepción Bay, two-thirds of the way down the peninsula, at precisely the same latitude as Florida's Sanibel Island two thousand miles to the east. Beneath us lay the Sea of Cortés, or Gulf of California, which separates Baja from the mainland of Mexico. This legendary body of water, once famous for its pearls and still a paradise for big-game fishermen and marine biologists, has had many names over the centuries. Juan Colorado, whose story was told by Charles Nordhoff, Sr., in *The Journey of the Flame*, preferred to call it the Vermilion Sea, after the Colorado River, which enters it from the north: "At each tide this river thrusts up a curling wave twenty feet high, to drown man or boat, which, seeking to explore its unknown reaches, offends its virginity. On its banks are springs of cold crimson water, burning the flesh it touches; from this coloring comes the name I love—the Vermilion Sea." Looking backward through the plane window, I could trace dimly the vast curve of the shore and the delta of the Colorado receding into the distance. In early geological periods the sea extended much further inland, for this is a rising coastline, as we were to see so clearly on closer inspection of the beaches and offshore islands. As late as the eighteenth century Baja appears on some maps as an island. Biologically speaking, the southern part of the peninsula has indeed an island character. The gulf insulates it from Mexico proper: even the bird life is quite different from that of the mainland. Northward the barren mountains extend almost from sea to sea; the valleys between them cut across the narrow peninsula, draining east and west. Further south, isolated mountain masses tend to divide Baja into discrete habitats, leading to a high incidence of "endemism" —i.e., of local forms, confined to a single region. Most dramatic of these perhaps is the "boojum tree," which we were later to see, if not wholly to believe.

With a large-scale map on our knees we watched the panorama unroll like one of those Japanese landscape scrolls which, wherever one views it, seems always to make a balanced composition. Westward lay row upon row of red-brown volcanic mountains, relieved here and there by a hint of green in the dry washes at their feet; as we flew nearer we could make out an occasional crater. In the foreground, rocky headlands jutted into the gulf; now we were passing a deep bay, its shores unmarked by any habitation, its inner reaches outlined by a sliver of silver sand.

We saw only two signs of human activity. One end of the rugged island of San Marcos looked as if it were covered with talcum powder; as we flew over we made out the white slopes and loading dock of a gypsum mine. Further on we passed an ugly little town with the beautiful name of Santa Rosalía, backed by hills of yellow-green ore that feed a copper-mining operation. Then nothing for fifty-odd miles, till suddenly an oasis seemed to spring from the desert—a lagoon bordered by a luxuriant stand of date palms, beyond which stretched, parallel to the peninsula itself, a narrow deep-blue bay dotted with tiny islands. It could almost have been a mirage. But there on the hilltop stood the ancient mission church of Mulegé, with rooftops of the village showing among the palms; and a white sail moved slowly down the lagoon. Circling the bay, we dropped into a cactus-bordered airstrip far out in the desert, after a preliminary run to scare off any stray cows or goats (sometimes, the pilot told us, it took two or three passes to degoat the runway). Minutes later, we were back in the eighteenth century, except that we rode in an International Harvester Travelall truck instead of on a mule.

The ten miles into the town of Mulegé took us almost as long as the flight down the Gulf. We were in no hurry. Here was our first glimpse of the local flora and fauna: the delicate white petals of the prickly poppy along the roadside, the globe mallow and an unlikely-looking milkweed with orange blossoms, lark sparrows and three kinds of doves—the mourning dove we knew at home, the tiny tame ground dove, and the lovely white-winged dove of the desert—and, as we approached the town, the fruit trees introduced by the early missionaries: the pomegranate, the lofty date palm, the banana, and the mango. By the time we had reached our destination—a cottage inn at the entrance to Concepción Bay—we knew that we were in another world.

What would we not give to see a bit of North America as it appeared to the first explorers? Only dimly from the printed page, from a journal entry or a hasty sketch, can we construct a picture of what it must have been like and share for a moment their sense of wonder and delight. How did Baja look to Hernan Cortés when, having conquered Mexico, he set sail across the narrow sea that bears his name? How did it look to the Jesuits who, nearly two centuries after Cortés, managed at last to settle in this savage land? In upper California the answer must be pieced together in libraries from the written records: to conjure up El Camino Real while whizzing down the Los Angeles freeways would take stronger djin than most of us have in our bottles. Much of the lower peninsula, however, appears today as it did then. To the visitor from above the border, an unspoiled body of water such as Concepción Bay seems like a gift from another age. Its purity is the result not of formal protection but simply of bad roads. Six-lane progress has not reached so far; the speedway-beercan biome extends only a hundred miles or so below Tiajuana.

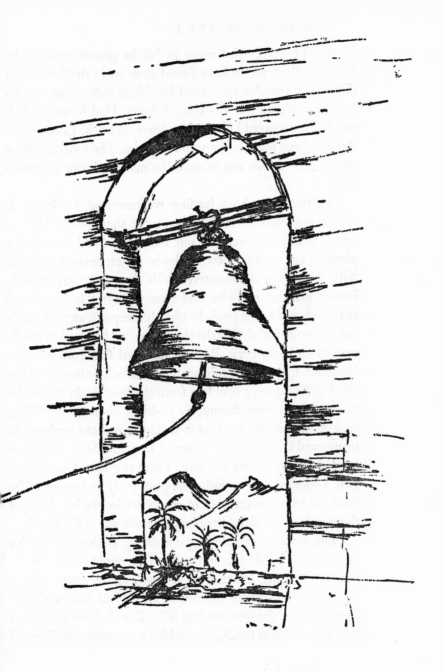

Henry Thoreau, who went to jail in protest against the Mexican War, might have found comfort in the fact that a diplomatic blunder prevented President Polk from acquiring the peninsula for the United States. Had he succeeded, the freeways would already be there. As it is, Concepción Bay has been given some years of grace. The morning after our arrival, we set out to make its more intimate acquaintance.

To reach the boat landing we traversed a salt marsh which is a favorite feeding place for shore birds. Willets (the western subspecies of our friends on Sanibel) raised a piercing cry as they flew restlessly about; several curlews, with their long down-curved bills, four magnificent red-brown marbled godwits, and a snowy egret had gathered at the edge of a tide pool. In slightly deeper water a Louisiana heron waded delicately along, leaning forward in readiness to strike its prey. Beyond the mud flats rose a rocky headland, topped by a miniature, box-like lighthouse; on the sheer cliffs below, a few feet from the boat dock, perched a raven eating a large shrimp, his jet-black plumage as striking against the pinkish rock as it would have been against the manicured lawns of the Tower of London. And as the boat headed slowly down the bay, I saw my first Heermann's gull, a handsome bird with slate-gray body and snow-white head, which we were later to encounter by the hundreds of thousands on its island breeding grounds out in the Gulf.

The sinuous shorelines gave direct evidence that this rugged land is rising from the sea. One could make out the traces of earlier shorelines, as one can in parts of the Nevada desert, where the rim of an ancient lake is clearly discernible on the surrounding hills. The shallow caves high above the present beach, formed by wave action millions of years ago, reminded us of caverns, similarly formed, that we had seen on the slopes of Isle Royale. An occasional patch of gleaming white sand had been molded by the wind into a ripple pattern of low dunes. Above each headland circled scores of frigate birds, their long, angled wings in black silhouette against a pale-blue sky, scissor-like tails opening and closing as they glided on the rising thermals. All were males, indicating that the females were on their nests some-where nearby. Offshore a roiling in the water turned out to be a school of porpoises, their dorsal fins slicing the surface in a sequence of lazy arcs.

As we had remarked when camping on St. John, the edge between sea and land on a tropical desert coast is strangely sharp. In the north we are accustomed to a transition zone between the two elements: broad salt marshes reclaimed by the sea at every high tide, fingers of the ocean reaching rhythmically landward, rivers whose lower stretches respond to the sea's pulse, their waters blending imperceptibly from fresh to salt. Sand bars come and go, fog drifts inland to modify the climate and the vegetation. But in Baja one wades ashore into a true desert.

Today the cove where we landed was bright with the yellow flowers of the paloverde, a delicate shrub whose green bark contrasted with the almost birch-white palo-blanco growing on the same slopes. The crescent beach of coarse shell sand—which blows about much less than the fine sand of our northern Atlantic beaches—was backed by an undercut cliff of volcanic rock, providing the only spot of shade. Here among the flotsam lay the carapace of a tortoise and the sun-baked remains of a large triggerfish with its surprisingly man-like teeth. Well above the water's

edge, supported by a cairn of loose rocks, rose a rough cross of weathered boards, the grave of a drowned fisherman. To the untrained observer it was the only reminder of human life. But a scientist in our party knew better. Within ten minutes he had discovered an ancient kitchen midden—a mound of broken clamshells into which he began to burrow happily, sieve in hand, in search of shards and traces of charcoal from campfires that had burned away before the dawn of history. Leaving him to his detective work, my wife and I turned inland to explore the cardon forest.

"Forest" requires a footnote. Get out of your head the idea of towering trunks and leafy canopies, of crowded vegetation and shelter from the sun. The cardon is a cactus, similar to the saguaro of our Southwest but with upraised rather than outstretched arms. "A gigantic plant," writes the Jesuit missionary Clavijero. "Grooved, thorny, leafless, upright, and parallel branches . . . grow from its thick trunk. . . . They grow to the height of even forty feet, and are thick (in proportion) and uniform from the trunk to their tips. . . . The Indians used the spines of this plant as fishhooks. Combs are made from the burr-like fruit, and the seeds are ground into flour for making cakes." Scattered over the desert, each of these "trees" needs plenty of space: not for sunlight, which is in oversupply, but for water, gathered from a wide area by the shallow roots and stored through months of drought in the leathery trunk. The struggle for life here is less obvious than in a northern forest. There the competition is for the sunlight, and the losers, overtopped by their neighbors, may stand dead or dying for years before they eventually fall to the forest floor. Though desert plants are fiercely armed with spikes and sabers against their animal foes (to whom they are so openly exposed), the battle between plant and plant goes on largely underground. To visualize the plant life of a desert, turn the whole landscape upside down in your mind's eye. The roots then become a tangled web of interlocking branches in a nightmare forest as luxuriant as the visible desert is sparse.

When so much is hidden, it is sometimes hard to believe that a desert shrub is alive. We wondered at the flaming flowers of the ocatillo or desert candle, bursting improbably from dead-looking limbs. The desert, like the arctic, represents a frontier in life's ceaseless and infinitely ingenious campaign to colonize every available inch of the planet. Where nothing else grows you will find lichens, forerunners of higher plants, first link in an endless chain. The life cycle of the flowering plants in both the arctic and the desert must be adjusted to a long period of dormancy followed by an explosive burst of speed: in the one case to take full advantage of the short summer, in the other to use to the utmost the unpredictable rain that may be followed by months or even years of drought. In terms of rainfall or snowfall, much of the arctic is indeed a desert, but the comparatively light precipitation is preserved by the cool summers and storage of water above the permafrost. In the southern desert it is more often a case of feast or famine. A cloudburst will deluge the hard-baked soil with more water than it can absorb and utilize: the run-off is not only useless to the plants but can cause vast damage, as we saw in the case of the old town of Mulegé, ever subject to disastrous floods by the river that gives it life.

More than any other, a desert landscape changes form and color with the angle of the sun. By the time we had finished exploring and sketching in the cardon forest, shadows and highlights had re-created in bold relief weird shapes of rock and plant that had been flattened by the vertical glare of noon, while the mountain peaks on the horizon had become sharply articulated in glowing red. The bay itself was rich in color and contrast, showing that

clear line between the green shallows and violet depths characteristic of tropic seas. The breeze dropped with the sun; frigate birds no longer circled the headlands. It had been a strange and haunting day, but stranger things were still to come.

Among the many oddities of Baja California the oddest of all is the previously mentioned "boojum tree," *Idria columnaris.* In *The Forgotten Peninsula,* Joseph Wood Krutch devotes an entire chapter to this unique aberration on the part of the Creator, which (with the exception of one small spot on the mainland of Mexico) is confined to a narrow section of Baja. Next morning found us flying north in our amphibious plane, headed for Los Angeles Bay, whence an hour's ride by truck would take us to the heart of a boojum forest. From the air the dark-blue bay looked like a model harbor, deep and curving and sheltered at its mouth by a scattering of small islands. Here lies a little village whose principal industry is the harpooning and sale of giant sea turtles. The air strip, running between a row of houses and the turtle shed, serves also as a sort of town plaza and playground: our plane had no sooner rolled to a stop than it was surrounded by a swarm of small boys, who shortly settled down to a game of marbles under the shadow of the wing. At the end of the plaza stood an exquisite little stone chapel faced with onyx. Flanking the doorway, like modern creations of abstract sculpture, lay two enormous whale vertebrae, bleached to a chalky white. White, too, was the cool interior, still decorated with white flowers from a wedding the previous day.

The next lap of the journey was rough. I had noticed heavy steel struts reinforcing the body of our truck, and I now understood why. This bit of El Camino Real is happily unimproved. It climbs every hillock and plunges into every dry wash, as it twists between outcroppings of red-brown rock. The desert floor itself is sandy and the vegetation full of variety: two species of ocatillo, distinguished from each other by the pattern of their branching; delicate smoke trees; dark gray ironwoods; cupals or incense trees, whose twigs have a spicy fragrance when you break them between your fingers; squat, grotesque elephant trees, named for the heavy tapering branches which are supposed to suggest an elephant's trunk, though to me their pattern seemed more like that of an octopus. Only more fantastic is the tree we had come especially to see.

One's first sight of a boojum inevitably evokes what Joe Krutch calls "the rustic-seeing-his-first-giraffe syndrome." In fact, if you can imagine a giraffe's neck projecting straight up out of the ground, you have a fair approximation of the simplest form of boojum, tapering skyward from a thick base, sometimes with a bunch of flowers bursting from its head. Other trees are more complicated, sprouting arms and hooks like surrealist hatracks. When we brought the truck to a lurching halt in this nightmare forest and began to explore on foot, we had a startling experience. In this remote desert, miles from any habitation, we came upon a single, neatly cut stump of a giant boojum. The botanist in the company did a double-take; then suddenly smiled in comprehension. Collected by a recent scientific expedition, this particular boojum now resides in the Smithsonian Institution in Washington, D.C.

Scientifically the boojum is closely related to that wide-ranging species, the ocatillo: its flowers, though whitish rather than burning red, are similar in structure, and both plants have a curious way of producing thorns from the stalks of their fallen leaves. Why the range of the boojum should be so restricted is still a mystery. It seems to grow well enough in cultivation. When at last we had left our boojum forest and jounced back over that roller-coaster road to Los Angeles Bay, I took a last look at the little onyx chapel before getting into the plane. Where suburbanites in the United States would have used cedar or arborvitae for their base planting, the people of Baja had quite properly used young boojums.

For sheer dramatic impact, we found nothing in Baja to compare with the offshore islands where the sea birds nest. These islands have all the romance of unexplored mountain peaks—which is exactly what many of them are. The absence of vegetation emphasizes this mountain character: bare cliffs rise sheer from the water's edge, often cut in at the base where new caves are slowly being formed in the softer rock by the incessant action of the waves. Other caverns, dating from an earlier geological age and now high above sea level, may be occupied by colonies of blue-footed boobies, their powder-blue feet bright against the white line of the nest's edge; a lower slope will be dotted with brooding pelicans, while ravens perch on the rocks above, waiting to pounce on an unprotected egg. An ordinary-looking island, when seen from the air, will reveal at its center a perfect crater, the top of a dead volcano. On any one of them the naturalist may find a surprise, such as the brown boobies, characteristic of the South Pacific, that we found nesting among the expected blue-footed species. For these are uncut pages in the book; new types of plants, possibly even of animals, may be still awaiting discovery.

Of the islands that we visited the most exciting was neither particularly scenic nor unexplored. Too small to appear on most maps, Isla Raza lies approximately between Los Angeles Bay and that ancient pirate stronghold, the large island of Tiburón. To bird-lovers it is of supreme importance as the only known breeding ground of the elegant tern, the western counterpart of the handsome royal and Caspian terns known to eastern bird-lovers. Our object was to check up on the present state of this unique colony. For here, on a wild spot far from any human dwelling, is a scene of incredible abundance. And here in brutal clarity lies the shadow of future extinction.

The shores of Raza consist of black volcanic rock, jagged and pockmarked like clinkers fresh from some Gargantuan furnace, splashed everywhere with white bird droppings. In the absence of sandy beaches, our amphibious plane anchored well out in deep water, and we rowed ashore two by two in a rubber life raft, to the sound of moaning seals on a nearby islet. Our arrival was not unobserved. Though supposedly Raza belonged only to the elegant terns and their natural rivals, the even more abundant Heermann's gulls, we had just had an ominous warning that all was not well. From the air we had been startled to see several dories with outboard motors drawn up on the mud flats of a tidal lagoon. Now their owners, a wild and tattered but not unfriendly crew, stood looking down on us, some of them barefoot on the sharp rocks, one holding a fish spear in his right hand and a still-flapping grouper in his left. Wading ashore, we picked our way among the slippery, kelp-covered boulders to the mud flat and the nearest dory. The owner stepped up and proudly lifted a cover of damp burlap sacking. The floor of the dory was already a foot deep in gull and tern eggs. We thought of Audubon's *Eggers of Labrador*. We thought of the extinct great auk. But today we weren't concerned with the dismal record of the past. Our job was to study the page that lay open before us.

Obviously the gulls and terns choose Raza because it is the one comparatively flat island among its larger and steeper companions, whose cliffs and elevated caves provide nesting sites for the pelicans and boobies. About twelve hundred feet wide, without shade or fresh water, it is built of three layers of volcanic rock which have become uptilted to produce three long ridges, between which lie the sandy flats where most of the birds nest. ("Nest" is a misleading term; eggs are laid in slight depressions in the sand, in the case of the gulls never less than two feet apart, but with the terns much closer.) This year there were perhaps half a million birds on the island: four hundred thousand gulls and between fifty and a hundred thousand terns (including some royal terns among the elegants). As we stepped ashore, our noses were assaulted with the ammoniac smell of guano, reminding us that the island had once been the scene of an ill-fated attempt to exploit this natural fertilizer; the business failed when a supply boat broke down and twelve men perished of thirst and starvation. The present incumbents, who numbered about twenty, were obviously not starving. Some were eating tortillas, and the litter around their camp indicated a varied menu, including three young ospreys.

Followed by several members of this ragged crew, to whom our motives were obscure and hence suspect, we climbed the nearest ridge. It formed a watershed, not of rivers but of birds. The flat to our right was speckled with thousands of gulls, to our left lay a shimmering blanket of terns. The chorus of sound was sharply divided: into one ear poured the gulls' plaintive mewing, into the other the terns' shrill cry. The birds ignored our presence; for a moment peace reigned. Then suddenly from behind us came a sort of rebel yell as the egg collectors charged down the slope, waving their arms and shouting into the midst of the nesting terns. The very ground seemed to rise as myriads of birds took to the air in wild alarm, shrieking and swirling about our heads in a blizzard of wings. Pails in hand, six or eight men fanned out over the flat to snatch every tern egg before the waiting gulls could swoop down to join in the plunder. It was a clean sweep: minutes later the pails were full and every nest was empty.

Such was the daily routine. The Heermann's gulls, themselves predators on the terns, suffered the same fate. Though they nested everywhere on the rocky slopes as well as on the flats, we could find, on exploring the rest of the island, only a handful of eggs and—almost unbelievably—not a single live chick. As we made our way back to the waiting plane, we wondered how any living creature, however abundant, could survive such exploitation.

A partial answer came two months later when a return expedition revisited Raza on June 7 (about seven weeks after the eggers left) to check up on the results of the spring nesting season. For the Heermann's gulls it had been a 99 per cent failure. Though the island was covered with adult birds, still in pairs at their nest scoops, the few young were less than a week old. In other words, during the time the eggers were on the island the destruction had been complete, and the colonies had never recovered. The terns had fared much better. Apparently they had still been able to lay and to incubate normally after the eggers had departed; though their numbers were smaller than in years back, they had managed to survive another season in the struggle for survival.

Are they fighting a losing battle? To us the ominous note on Raza was not the men but the outboard motors. Egging has gone on in Baja California since time immemorial, as it has for example among the coastal Eskimos of Alaska, and the birds in each case have survived. When does legitimate harvest become exploitation? Modern weapons and modern machinery have forced the issue everywhere in the world, from the arctic ice floes to the tropical deserts, from the sky above us to the ocean floor. Isla Raza is a tiny but significant case in point. As I write, a plan is being discussed with the Mexican government to save its birds from annihilation. If this succeeds, conservation will have won another skirmish in the endless battle to save our natural heritage, and the Vermilion Sea preserved a treasure perhaps as precious as its now vanished pearls.

CHAPTER 14

Family Safari

WHEN I told my eleven-year-old daughter—a great lover of animals of every size shape and composition—that we were planning a family camping trip in the wilds of East Africa, she went straight to the attic and retrieved a well-loved, ragged leopard, to renew his acquaintance before leaving. It was a happy omen. Nine months later, at dusk on the edge of the great Serengeti Plain, a dream came to life. We (my wife, son, and two daughters and I) had already been ten days on safari and had seen an enormous variety of game, but the secretive leopard was a prize that had eluded us. Now, perhaps because I had

((203

given up seriously searching, my eye was caught by a strange shape that seemed to grow from the lower limb of a fever tree above the river. In the binoculars the lump became the body of a large leopard stretched along the limb, its legs and tail dangling down on either side as if all the stuffing had gone out of it. While we strained our eyes in the fading light it slowly stretched awake; its day was beginning as ours, with the suddenness of nightfall in the tropics, came to an end. Reluctantly we returned to camp. Where would "our" leopard be tomorrow?

Next morning we were out well before daylight. Two dik-diks zigzagged like rabbits in the headlights of the Land-Rover. As the east reddened, a fine herd of eland with their heavy dewlaps and back-curving horns marched in awesome silhouette against the sunrise. Flocks of sand grouse flew down to the river to drink. Three hyenas, easy to spot with their sloping backs and short rocking gait, ran purposefully across the plain, one with a small gazelle in its mouth. And the leopard? The sun was already two hours up, and our hearts were down, when a magnificent form appeared not ten yards in front of the car, walking with soft lithe grace, head turning neither right nor left. Cautiously we circled around ahead of her (it was a female), taking our station near the foot of a wide-spreading umbrella acacia that we guessed might be her chosen hideout for the day. On she came, apparently oblivious to our presence. At the base of the tree she paused, seemed about to go on, then to our joy bounded up the trunk, and methodically sniffed along each limb until her bedroom was thoroughly explored. Well fed after her night's hunt, she deliberately draped herself over a lower branch in full view of the cameras that our son, the photographer of the party, had trained upon her. Head resting on paws, she roused herself reluctantly for a last look around, and closed her eyes in sleep.

It was an almost domestic scene, yet it was wholly wild: wild in the sense that human beings had no impact on it. We were privileged witnesses only, come to observe the great beasts going about their business as if we did not exist. In few parts of the world is this still possible; East Africa is one of them. Here geography has been on the side of the animals. Remoteness, inaccessibility, ruggedness of terrain, the malaria mosquito deadly to man and the tsetse fly fatal to domestic cattle: these have kept some of Africa's best game country outside the white man's pattern of conquest. Kenya and Tanganyika, through which we were now traveling, were still wholly unexplored when the fate of our own Wild West was sealed with the driving of the Golden Spike. The country belonged to the animals and to the native tribes such as the Masai, who, like our Plains Indians, lived among them in mutual tolerance. Today, with modern means of transport, with expanding native population, with all the technical devices at man's disposal for subduing his environment, even this last outpost of Eden is at bay. There is only one hope for its survival: our awaking conscience toward our fellow creatures on this planet, our growing sense of trusteeship for a natural heritage which we did not create, and which is not ours to destroy. In practical terms, this means protection by law not only of the animals themselves but of their homeland; in most cases it is the habitat rather than the species itself that is in danger of extinction. It means understanding the complex relationship between one animal and another and between each and its environment, and establishing parks and equivalent reserves adequate to preserve their way of life.

During a month's safari one can at most sample the riches of the remaining African wilderness, represented by the great herds of migratory ungulates or hoofed mammals, with their predators and scavengers, that were common to most continents within historical times. In the words of a leading authority, Lee M. Talbot, "one of the last places where this phenomenon can still be seen is in the region of the Serengeti National Park in Tanganyika and the adjoining Mara Masai Reserve area of Kenya." It was on the Mara River that we made our first camp.

We had flown overnight from London to Nairobi, the capital of Kenya, which lies in high, cool country less than two degrees below the Equator—today an aggressively modern city on one of the world's principal air routes. Here our safari began. (Anywhere you go in Africa beyond the corner drugstore is a safari, so long as it involves camping; when you stay at inns or lodges it is a "tour.") There were the five members of our family, our Kenyaborn English guide, four young Kikuyus, tents, cots, food for the first two weeks, four cameras, six pairs of binoculars, tape recorder, butterfly net, a rifle for emergencies, several drums of petrol, and miscellaneous spare parts—all packed into three Land-Rovers like fishhooks in a tackle box. The first part of our course lay northwestward to Lake Nakuru, famous for its flamingos, thence south on a dirt track through the high Mau forest and westward to the Mara River.

Though mid-July is a dry season, light rain (need I say?) was falling when we left the old Norfolk Hotel, traditional starting point for East African safaris. Not till

we reached the precipitous drop-off into the Great Rift Valley did the sun break through and the landscape broaden out, layer after layer through the slowly dissolving mist, giving us the feeling, as Isak Dinesen puts it in *Out of Africa*, that we were living up in the air: "The views were immensely wide. Everything that you saw made for greatness and freedom, and unequaled nobility." The vegetation along the roadside was as compelling in its way as the distant hills—the euphorbia candelabra with its spread of upright cactus-like branches, the Cape chestnut, covered with broad pink blossoms, the purple flowering jacaranda, and one magnificent avenue of flame trees. By lunchtime we were parked in the long grass on the shore of Lake Nakuru.

Thanks largely to the ornithologist Roger Tory Peterson, Lake Nakuru is now a national park, and it makes a dazzling introduction to the bird life of East Africa (which comprises over a thousand species—more than twice as many as in North America east of the Rockies). Here were yellow-billed storks, sacred ibis, black-winged stilts, rafts of ducks. A dead tree overhanging the water was festooned with white pelicans, reminding us of the mangroves of Sanibel Island flowering with white ibis. Dominating all were the flamingos—bright pink against the pale-blue waters of the lake, glowing a deeper red as they took to the air. It was too much to be real: we were with Alice in Wonderland, and if the flamingos had all turned into croquet mallets we would have taken it in our stride.

This sense of unreality remained as we drove through rolling farmland that might have been in Pennsylvania—with cottages and churches straight out of England—only to find ourselves a few hours later in dense jungle with red-headed parrots screaming overhead and black-and-white Colobus monkeys swinging in the treetops. I remember particularly the shy bushbuck at evening in a glade by the river where we washed off the red dust of the first day's journey, and at night the ear-splitting scream of a little mammal called the tree hyrax, a sound which has been said to start like a creaky door and end like a baby being strangled.

This is Masai country, and the Masai are great walkers. On the next day's drive from the Mau forest to the Mara River, I think we met only two or three other vehicles, but a handsome variety of pedestrians. Slim, almost slight, the Masai warrior (who lives on a diet of blood and milk) has the sort of sinewy strength that does not show itself in bulging biceps and muscular calves. His features too tend to be delicate. The high-bridged nose, the sensitive mouth, do not look negroid; one young warrior who later visited our camp might have come straight out of an Egyptian painting. The basic costume was a brick-red cloth (still called "mericani" from the early American traders) around the waist, a blanket over one shoulder, and a spear. The young warrior's pride—and badge of his bachelorhood—is his hairdo: a mat of fine twists plastered with clay and red ocher, parted sidewise from ear to ear, falling backward over his neck and forward to a point in the middle of his forehead. One small boy on the road was magnificently gotten up, with stripes of white clay down his legs, cowrie-shell ornaments, and a broad round hat decorated with ostrich feathers and a brim of tiny sunbirds which he had shot himself (with a blunt-tipped arrow) as part of the circumcision rites into manhood.

The Masai girls shave their heads, and very charming

they are with their beautifully rounded skulls. Naked above the waist, they are laden with armbands and leg-bands; loops and pendants in their fantastically enlarged ear lobes (which the men have as well) and above all heavy necklaces of bright beads and wire, in concentric layers like the rings of Saturn. But the nicest thing about a Masai girl is her smile. At the village where we stopped to fill our gasoline tanks for the last time, we got a warm welcome when our nationality became known. The local school had been built with American aid.

The Masai tribe have a quality rare in the modern world: they don't like possessions. With one unfortunate exception. To the Masai man, cattle are wealth; with them he buys wives to work for him (one marriageable young warrior, with a twinkle in his eye, offered me twenty cows for my older daughter) and his status depends in large measure on the size of his herd. Quantity not quality counts; like worn dollar bills, scrawny cows are legal tender. To the conservationist the Masai's role in Africa today is am-bivalent. Feared by the agricultural tribes, they have helped to save the game by preserving the land from cultivation and hunting. Yet as their herds and flocks increase they overgraze the range, competing with the wild animals and turning grassland into desert.

Our first day in the bush, some eighty miles north of where we saw the leopard, is etched in my memory with the vividness of any first impression. The previous evening we had turned off the dirt track onto what our guide called a "secondary road"—two wheel marks barely visible in the high grass. We had crossed a swamp and pitched our tents on the bank of the Mara River, in a grove of trees which hung out in a mass of tangled roots over the swirling coffee-colored water. Though there were probably no other human beings within fifty miles, heaps of elephant

droppings on our doorstep indicated that we were not without neighbors. A few yards upstream, where the bank sloped more gradually into a deep pool, the churned-up mud told a fuller story. Mingled with the huge round tracks of elephant were others that we learned to distinguish: the rhino, with its three toe marks and the hippo with four, the hoofprints of buffalo exactly like those of domestic cattle, the colt-like track of zebra. The great cat-like impressions were the pug marks of a lion.

When darkness had fallen, we had listened to the hippos grunting and splashing in the river below and for an instant had caught two protruding eyes in the beam of our flashlight. During the night we had heard the distant roar of a lion and, startlingly close at hand, the lugubrious howl of hyenas. (Later we discovered they had made off with a cooking pot.) We were up an hour before sunrise. The stars were fading. A sliver of old moon, cusps pointing upward, shone against the reddening east. The birds were awakening. We heard the soft *ker-r-r ku-ku, ker-r-r ku-ku* of the ring-necked dove, which we came to associate with every camp site near water, and the raucous laugh of the beautiful hadada ibis. Silently a saddle-billed stork flew directly overhead. Though it was still too dark to distinguish colors, there was no mistaking this largest of African waders, more than five feet from bill tip to tail.

We had been warned that it can be cold on the Equator at over five thousand feet. Even with heavy sweaters, jackets, and mufflers, and fortified by hot tea, we were barely warm as we got into the Land-Rover and made for a bend in the river where we hoped to find last night's hippos. Leaving the car, we walked silently to the river's edge through knee-high grass drenched with dew. Presently in midstream appeared two sets of round ears and huge nostrils pointed skyward. With a great *whoosh!* of intaking breath, the hippos softly submerged, to appear again almost beneath our feet. On they came, adults and young, holding their own with miraculous ease against the strong current, raising their heads in colossal gaping yawns, sometimes climbing partway up the bank to feed on overhanging shrubs. At last they had all drifted downstream, apparently converging on their favorite pool for the day. Leaving the riverbank, we hastened to explore the open plain before all signs of last night's activities had vanished. The great mammals are largely nocturnal, and much of the relentless contest between predator and prey takes place in the dark. Though we had front-row seats, we were attending a play in which the curtain goes up on an empty, debris-littered stage, with confused sounds echoing from the wings. If we were lucky this morning, we might get a glimpse of some of the stragglers on the stage, or their fresh traces, from which we could reconstruct the previous evening's drama.

We were just in time. My older daughter, who became our champion "spotter," was standing in the open hatch of the Land-Rover as it lurched over trackless grassland like a small boat in a choppy sea. High up at nine o'clock (i.e., to the left, at right angles to our course) she made out a dozen tiny specks, circling and slowly descending. They could only be vultures, probably dropping down to a kill. As a wheeling flock of gulls and terns will lead the deep-sea fisherman to a school of feeding fish, so will soaring vultures betray the scene of battle in the bush. Turning in their direction, we drove ahead as fast as we dared, stopping now and then to scan the ground through our binoculars; the vultures had landed, but where? Suddenly a ragged black wing rose out of the tawny plain. Driving closer, we came on a classic scene in the life-and-death drama, the last act before the curtain rings down. Upon the trampled grass lay a dismembered carcass, identifiable by the horns as a wildebeest, favorite prey of lions. A hooded vulture was perched on the head, tearing at the remaining flesh with prodigious strength; others were piling one on another as they fought for bits and pieces. A spotted hyena, his face bloody to the ears, loped off with a leg as we approached; equipped with jaws even stronger than a lion's, he is the champion bone-crusher among the scavengers. Two silver-backed jackals—the common plains species—lurked on the outskirts of the fray, darting in and out with the quick steps of light, graceful dogs. A side-striped jackal—a handsomer, more wolf-like animal with bushy white-tipped tail—gnawed methodically on the rib case. Contesting his rights was a solitary lappet-faced vulture. Far larger and rarer than the hooded, he looked almost handsome in his dark-brown plumage and ruff below his purplish head and face. Each time the vulture tried to horn in, the jackal drove him off, but I noticed that both species of vulture fed amicably side by side. Attractive or not, the scavengers are the essential sanitary corps of the African plain, and the speed and thoroughness of their work is phenomenal. Some days later, we came upon a fresh zebra kill during our morning rounds. When we returned later in the day, all that remained to mark the spot was a single vulture feather and a bloodstain on the grass.

The sun by now was well above the horizon; we began peeling off jackets and sweaters as we drove on through terrain as various as it was vast. Groves of scrubby thorn trees, looking gray and dead during this dry season, alternated with open golden plains, shaded here and there with feathery umbrella acacias. These in turn gave way to wastes where the Masai had been burning the grass—some of the older burns already washed with bright green as the new growth returned, assuring the Masai of good grazing if drought should ever force them to turn their cattle into this area. Hidden rocks and invisible potholes lent a sporting element to our errant progress. One moment the landscape seemed utterly lifeless; then over the next rise would appear a dense herd of zebra, giving their sharp dog-like bark as they ran, never away from us, but diagonally in front of the car.

Everywhere were antelopes, some shy, some surprisingly approachable, bounding off a few yards and stopping, torn between wariness and curiosity over the strange but apparently harmless shape in their midst. We soon learned to identify them at a considerable distance: the ubiquitous little tommy with his broad black side stripe; the larger, white-rumped Grant's gazelle; the high-shouldered, long-faced kongoni, with its unique bracket-shaped horns. The somewhat similar topi, common here though gone from most of Kenya, we recognized by his short backswept horns and glossy coat with black patches on forelegs and thighs—which I at first assumed were the result of rolling in the burnt grass! Several times during the morning we met a topi standing guard on one of the great termite mounds that rise above the plain, and once we watched a butting contest between two males: a strictly formal duel in which, after coming together with an audible crash, each contestant would pause to survey the landscape for possible danger before returning to the fray. Of all the antelopes, we agreed that the high-bounding impala was the most spectacularly beautiful: the male in his proud spread of horns, set off by his harem (we once counted as many as fifty) of demure, hornless females.

We had seen the remains of a wildebeest; now against the horizon there were hundreds of black shapes inching forward in single file, unmistakable in the outline of their massive heads and shoulders, at a distance more suggestive of the American bison than of an antelope, to which family they in fact belong. More than any other animal, the wildebeest gave me a sense of the vast difference between the appearance of a wild creature in confinement and in its own domain. A captive wildebeest or gnu is something of a monstrosity, a freak for children to gape at, with its great shaggy head and long white beard, its homely face and spindly legs. The same animal galloping lightly across the plain, or whirling and prancing in sudden alarm, is the embodiment of alertness and grace. And so of the giraffe, whose long neck is anything but comical when you see him feeding, as we did this morning, from the top of a thorn tree; indeed one has not seen a giraffe at all until one has watched a herd of adults and young galloping like a film in slow motion, necks undulating in rhythm with their effortless gait. Today we were twice blest when we came on a group of giraffes with nursing young: utterly delightful replicas of their elders but sporting bushier manes and shaving brushes where their horns were to be.

The great concentration of wildebeest in their mass migrations may most nearly duplicate the limitless abundance that once characterized the American West. Nevertheless I think that a galloping herd of African buffalo best gives the sense of sheer unswerving power that, according to early travelers, was the most awesome thing about the American bison. Once found in vast numbers throughout East Africa, the buffalo were almost wiped out in the 1890's by an epidemic of rinderpest, the disease carried by domestic cattle. Their recovery since that time is cited as an example of the remarkable resilience of wild animals. Today there are several herds of over five hundred buffalo in the area where we were camped, and it was our good fortune to come across one such herd before the morning was out. Cantering up a shallow defile at right angles to our path, they streamed in front of the car, several animals abreast, in an undulating black river, dust rising from pounding hooves, close enough so that we could pick out the old bulls with the greatest expanse of horn (the record heads come from this region) and note the browner tinge of the calves, who seemed generally to keep toward the center of the mass. Reaching the end of the defile, the herd spread out like a giant delta, slowly losing momentum as it climbed the gentle slope beyond. So we left them grazing among the scattered acacias, grateful to them for a display which is all too rare since man has tamed the earth.

By the time we returned to camp, the sun was almost overhead and the massive fig tree above our camp table was humming with insects. In the tropics the noon hour is a time for "green thoughts in a green shade"; only mad dogs and Englishmen—and lepidopterists—go out in the midday sun. This is the time when the butterflies are on the wing. An enthusiastic if spasmodic collector since childhood, I was overwhelmed with the glorious variety of giant swallowtails and *Charaxes* that congregated wherever there was a sunny opening in the jungle—too often, alas, flitting high amid the treetops. We must have made an odd picture: me with my collecting net, our guide walking ahead with his heavy double-barreled rifle—since the only paths were tunnel-like trails used by elephant, buffalo, and rhino. Early afternoon was the time for bathing and fishing. I say "bathing" rather than swimming, since we confined our ablutions to the occasional rocky rapids where crocodiles were unlikely to lurk. The fishing was fruitful. From a deep pool I took in half an hour enough catfish for supper: hideous-looking creatures but quite sporting on a fly rod, and superb eating, their bellies stuffed with the ripe figs that dropped into the river from the overarching trees.

Our evening excursion was on foot. In the African national parks, one must stay in one's car except at a campground, but we were now in a game reserve and could walk wherever we pleased. Our guide was permitted to carry a gun, though there would have been a whopping fine if he had had to use it. Walking among wild animals is quite a different sensation from seeing them from a vehicle. Among an unknown number of creatures who may not wait to learn that your intentions are peaceful, you are aware of being a relatively weak and slow-moving mammal, with fair eyesight but a deficient sense of smell. For example, we took care not to arouse the maternal wrath of the herd of a dozen elephants and young that we presently found feeding at the edge of the forest. Silently we approached upwind across the open plain; an elephant's hearing and smell are acute, but it is very shortsighted. One of the cows was reaching high up with her trunk to break off whole branches of an acacia which she was stuffing into her mouth, another was suckling a charming little baby from the teats between her forelegs. Two bulls were playing a rather rough game, not so much a butting as a shoving contest, forehead to forehead and tusk to tusk. Since the wind was puffy, likely to shift any instant, we dared not approach too close; when the nearest elephant began flapping its ears and nervously sniffing the air with its trunk, we beat a strategic retreat. (Two days later, at dawn, a herd of at least thirty elephants of all ages almost stumbled into our camp by their waterhole, to their intense irritation. Our retreat on that occasion was less deliberate.)

Continuing upstream, we came upon four shy water-buck, easily identified by their dark color and rather square profile. On the borders of a swamp a group of crowned cranes were engaged in their courtship dance, the low sun shining on their golden heads, suggesting the song and dance routine of Masai warriors. In the swamp itself a jacana or lily-trotter, bright chestnut with powder-blue forehead, stepped delicately upon the floating lily pads between flowers of violet-blue, while above the river hovered a pied kingfisher, its arrow bill pointed straight down toward its quarry. The snowy-headed fish eagle on a snag above the water reminded us of our national bird, though his russet-brown shoulders made him almost more handsome. While we were watching him a Schalow's touraco—a crested, bright-green bird with crimson flight feathers—landed above our heads and scampered along a branch with its characteristic squirrel-like gait.

In the river itself we found no crocodiles—only their fresh tracks in the sand—but we had a quick glimpse of a monitor lizard as it scurried away: four or five feet long, it must be the nearest thing to a dragon outside the story-

books. By now the sun was an orange disk, glowing faintly through the smoke of grass fires. Reluctantly we turned homeward, risking a short cut through the forest along a tortuous track that smelled like a zoo. As with the grizzly bears in Alaska, the idea at such times is to avoid taking your host by surprise; we therefore sang and shouted until we emerged once more into the open plain. Here we had a last bit of luck: a close view through our binoculars of the elusive white-spotted stone curlew, a bird of nocturnal habits which is seldom seen by day. Back in camp, we listened to baboons barking and watched a group of slender, long-tailed vervet monkeys silhouetted in a bare tree against the fading light. As darkness fell, ribbons of red flickered across the horizon. Far off, a lion roared. The cycle had ended and begun.

Africa and the African lion are inseparable. Of all the great beasts, it is the one that arouses the most curiosity, the most awe, and probably the most affection. It is also, from the safety of a Land-Rover, the easiest of all animals to observe at close range. During our trip we encountered lions in all sizes and combinations: solitary males, two males sharing a kill, a pride of young lions rousing them-selves for the evening hunt, a mated pair on their "honey-moon" (during which they keep to themselves and fast for several days), a pride of several families feeding on a zebra and another with young in the kitten stage, alter-nately roughhousing and nursing. The incident I treasure most occurred one morning on the open plain. What looked like a stump in the long grass turned out to be the head of a splendid male lion, resting in the sun after a successful night's hunt. As he moved slowly off in a straight line we circled ahead to take our stand near his path. We saw him pass within a few yards of a herd of zebra and topi; instead of running away, they actually made short dashes *toward* him, apparently aware that his belly was full but anxious nevertheless to keep him in sight. By now we saw his objective: another mature male with an even fuller, dark-tipped mane, waiting sleepily in the grass. Approaching him, the first lion broke into a trot and joined his friend with a great display of affection. They rubbed necks and tumbled about with feet in air, finally passing not five yards from the car and settling down side by side, heads swaying in unison, eyes closed to the sun.

Emblem of royalty, the lion has nevertheless been considered vermin when he interfered with the spread of civilization; at the turn of the century, for example, the Uganda Railway was paying a bounty on lions, and many more were slaughtered in the name of sport. Nor do they recover quickly; a lioness in the wild gives birth only every two or two and a half years, and seldom do all the young survive to maturity. Today experts rank the lion as one of the animals threatened with extinction in Kenya, along with the rhinoceros and cheetah and wild dog; estimates indicate that there are less than a thousand individuals left in this major reservoir of African wildlife.

Indeed, many of East Africa's finest mammals are in a critical situation. The decline of the black rhinoceros—which may well go the way of its Asian cousins—represents a tragic combination of inevitable conflict and senseless persecution. The friction between a dangerous animal and expanding population could not be avoided; in settled areas the rhino had to go. But today, when the pitiful remnant should be wholly protected, the rhino is the one species most seriously endangered by poaching. Rhino horn, supposedly endowed with aphrodisiac qualities, is literally worth its weight in gold in some parts of the Orient. To the conservationist, every living rhino is precious; hence the techniques that have been developed for transporting individuals from unprotected areas to the safety of the national parks. One of the novel experiences of our trip was the pursuit of a rhino, with cross-bow and arrow tipped with anesthetic, in the company of a game warden who has made a fine art of this rescue operation. When later we were charged by another rhino while in the comparative safety of a Land-Rover, I wished I knew how to tell him to relax, that we were really on his side.

Students of African wildlife are also deeply concerned —and puzzled—by the rapid decline of the cheetah. This slim, small-headed, leopard-like creature hunts by day. After tirelessly stalking its quarry the cheetah runs it down with an incredible burst of speed, estimated at over a mile a minute. Apparently never plentiful in East Africa, it is disappearing more rapidly than legal hunting or poaching could explain; naturalists suspect that it is subject to some unknown disease. One prays for its survival, for there are few more thrilling sights than a pair of hungry cheetahs out on a hunt. One day we approached a fine animal to within a few yards and listened to its sharp, bird-like cry, almost a whistle, strangely suggestive (though on a higher pitch) of the call note of the veery in our New England woods.

The wild dog, once considered the lowest of vermin, is also on the danger list today. In maintaining the ecological balance, in keeping the great herds of ungulates on the move, it serves the same purpose that the wolf formerly did on our Great Plains, and as he still does among the caribou herds of Canada and Alaska.

Some of the other smaller animals do much to enrich the African scene: the elusive bat-eared fox, the comical wart hog, with his grotesque tusks and tail held like a flagpole; the shy, exquisite bushbuck and the swift-footed duiker. Then there are those two inhabitants of the kopjes (pronounced "coppys") which rise like rocky islands in the sea of grass: the sure-footed little klipspringer, bounding like a goat on the tips of his toes, and the round, placid rock hyrax (close relative of the creature that had kept us awake in the Mau forest), resembling, in a family group, nothing so much as a scattered pile of boulders. All are part of the complex web of life which, in the areas we were visiting, still remains unbroken.

. . .

One of the joys of an East African safari lies in the infinite variety of the country itself. The first part of our trip, in the game reserves and parks of southern Kenya and Tanganyika, took us through high jungle at over nine thousand feet, through wind-swept plains where the trees on the horizon shimmered like a mirage; to the floor of Ngorongoro, the world's largest crater, where Masai warriors sang all afternoon into our tape recorder and at evening took us back to their village along with their lowing herds of cattle; to the famous park at Amboseli, below the snows of Kilimanjaro.

The second part, in the remoter areas of Kenya's Northern Frontier District, was wholly different. The nature of this harsh dry country, inhabited only by desert tribes, is shown by the designations on our map: "Very Broken Country," "Thorn Bush and Sand Plain, Occasional Lava," "Water by Digging," and (my favorite phrase) "Reported Route Passable to Camels." Here we found different races of the same animals we had come to know in the south: the Somali ostrich with his blue legs and jet-black wings, so much handsomer than his southern cousin; the Grant's zebra, larger and more finely striped than the common Chapman's; the reticulated giraffe, named for the net-like pattern of his markings; the gray beisa oryx, whose straight spear-sharp horns, like those of the more brownish subspecies to the south, can skewer a lion. And here flourishes that unbelievable antelope, the gerenuk (Somali for "giraffe-necked"), which stands on its hind legs to browse the "wait-a-bit" thorns and which never has to drink.

Camped on the only stream within at least a hundred miles, we learned—after one exhausting experience—to keep out of the blazing sun and confine our explorations, which we generally made on horseback, to early morning and to the two hours before dark. One morning as we were following an elephant track in the sand I was puzzled to hear a hollow musical murmur like a brook running over pebbles. A parade of gangling shapes blocked our path; the music resolved itself into scores of wooden camel bells. Twenty miles away, where the foraging was good, a tribe of the nomadic Rendile had established a village; twice a month they drove their camels to the water where we were encamped. These desert rivers have a strange pattern, bursting cold and clear out of the mountains to form cascades and rocky pools, then gradually disappearing into the sand; to find deep water you go upstream, not down. When we returned for breakfast we could hardly see the river for the camels. From then on we had to bathe and get our drinking water far upstream, but any inconvenience was more than balanced by the pleasure of having such attractive visitors as the spare, rugged Rendile. There seems to be something in living close to the bone that fosters friendliness to strangers. This was their country, and in a sense we were their guests: quite literally one night when they invited us to join them in a dance which consisted of holding hands in a circle (their girls are quite as charming as the Masai) and jumping up and down to the beat of a tireless chant, climaxing in a wild yell. During the day the warriors would lounge around camp leaning on their light spears (they generally carried two, on the double-barreled-rifle principle), dressing their hair, or bathing in the river—natural and unself-conscious in their nakedness, calling "Jambo!" to my wife as she walked along the bank.

If we were guests of the native people we were also exploring the country on the animals' own terms. This was brought home to us one evening with a certain emphasis. We were riding in single file up a sand river—roughly the equivalent of a dry wash in the American West. Rounding a bend, we suddenly came upon an old bull elephant, downwind. Forward went his great ears, up went his trunk in a blood-chilling scream as he made for us across the sand. Our ponies, who knew that signal, broke for the bush. As one barely able to stay on a horse when there are no elephants around, I lagged behind in this maneuver; and though my wife encouraged me by shouting "Don't fall off!" I was much relieved that the old bull's *amour-propre* did not oblige him to press home the charge. At a safe distance we stopped to look back: our host's bad temper was explained by a spear wound in his side, doubtless the work of a young warrior out to prove his manhood.

Despite the heavy trade in ivory of past years, and the poaching that still goes on, the elephant is one of the great animals that is holding its own wherever it is given a fair chance; the number in Kenya today is probably greater than it was fifty years ago. Again it is a matter of space: in some parts of Africa, where expanding settlement has driven the elephants to take refuge in the remaining protected areas, there is a denser population than the country can support.

All too soon it was time to head south for Nairobi. My thoughts naturally turned to the future: would later generations be able to enjoy what we had enjoyed, or was it all doomed in the sacred name of Progress? The disappearance of wild animals everywhere in the world has now assumed the proportions of a major crisis. The appalling aspect of the problem is the accelerated *rate* at which they are going. Of the hundred-odd species that have become extinct since the birth of Christ, seventy per cent have vanished in the last hundred years; since 1900 we have lost an average of *one species every year*.

The roster of threatened species is frighteningly long. The mammals alone, in a list recently compiled by the World Wildlife Fund, total over ninety species, from every continent. The great Indian rhinoceros is in far worse straits than its African cousin, being reduced to a few hundred individuals; the Javan and Sumatran species may well be doomed. The beautiful Arabian oryx, once distributed throughout the Middle East, has recently been slaughtered by motorized calvacades in the name of sport; desperate measures are now being taken to save it by starting a colony in Arizona. The Asiatic lion, referred to so often in the Bible, has vanished along with the disappearing wilderness; about three hundred now remain in a forest reserve under the enlightened protection of the Indian government. The mountain gorilla, recently the subject of intensive study, is making a last stand in the African Congo as its jungle habitat shrinks. The white-tailed gnu, which once roamed the South African plains in the millions, no longer exists in the wild. The polar bear, whose principal range is the North American arctic, and which has always played an important part in the Eskimo economy, is threatened as never before by "sportsmen" with air transport and high-powered rifles.

One could go on and on. To the list of mammals one could add an even longer list of birds that have vanished from the earth during historic times or that are now—like those two magnificent relics of our American past, the whooping crane and the California condor—reduced almost to the point of no return. But the picture is not wholly black. In America, for example, we did save the snowy egret and the wild turkey, the wood duck and the trumpeter swan; the fur seal once more breeds by the thousands on the Pribilof Islands; buffalo can at least be seen in our parks; and there is still hope for endangered species such as the bighorn sheep and the woodland caribou. We are even beginning to learn that the wolf, most maligned and misunderstood of creatures, plays a valuable part in the economy of the wild.

As the world awakens to the urgent need for conservation, all eyes are turned toward East Africa. These are the crucial years, when power is passing from the hands of colonial governments to the African people. Will they realize that their wild animals are among their greatest treasures? In the drive toward industry and modernization, will they recognize that the wild parts of Africa are not only a burgeoning source of tourist income but a spiritual inspiration to all mankind? There is reason to think that they may. Political leaders have issued strong statements endorsing conservation. National parks continue to receive financial support; a few new reserves, under local direction, are being established. Future administrators are being trained in game management and young Africans are being invited to America to study in our parks and universities. In East African towns films of local wildlife are being shown to men and women and children who may never in their lives have seen a giraffe or an elephant. These efforts have received strong support from America and Europe, as well they should, for the survival of our great beasts is a world concern. Henceforth the trustees will be the Africans themselves; but how effectively they discharge their trust will depend upon us all. When anyone asks me about the future, I think of that ubiquitous East African bird, the augur buzzard, so named because one's first sight of him in the morning determines one's fortunes for the day. If he is facing you, you will have good luck; if he turns his back, watch out! As I write, the sun is rising on a new Africa. I pray that the augur buzzard is looking us in the eye.

CHAPTER 15

Man and Wilderness

O N A N Y wilderness trip there comes a moment when you say to yourself: "What am I doing here?" As a matter of fact, throughout most of history what you are doing would have been considered sheer madness. The subject of civilized man vis-à-vis the natural world is as broad as all outdoors, but at least one can define its limits without going far afield. Take, at the one pole, the rejoinder of the famous Boston wit and scholar Helen Bell to a friend who innocently remarked, on a beautiful spring morning, that she was going for a walk in the country. "Well," said Mrs. Bell sourly, "kick a tree for me!" Mrs.

Bell was blood-sister to Hazlitt's cockney, who declared he would rather be hanged in London than die a natural death in the country. Take at the other pole Henry Thoreau, who despised cities and believed that "in wildness is the preservation of the world." Somebody said of Thoreau that he could get more out of ten minutes with a woodchuck than most men could get from a night with Cleopatra. These are the extremes. In any place and in any period there is obviously an infinite variety of individual attitudes toward nature, all the way from the gushing "Oh, the wonder of it" approach of sentimental "nature writers" to the laconic Englishman whose only comment on being shown the great fall of water at Niagara was: "What's to stop it?"

Leaving personal idiosyncrasies aside, it is possible to trace in broad outline the changing pattern of man's relationship to wild nature throughout history. As I said at the beginning, this is not merely an academic exercise. Only within our lifetime has technology and population pressure reached the point where absolute control—or, more accurately, absolute destruction—of the world's remaining wilderness becomes a real possibility. Our attitude is therefore a matter of immediate concern. What is that attitude, and where did it come from? Looking back, one can see it evolving through successive stages of fear, of identification, of patronizing and romanticizing, of conquest and exploitation, of scientific understanding, and finally of alarmed realization that there are few wild areas left on the globe.

Our Western cultural tradition, particularly in its Old Testament origins, has a different concept of nature from that of the East. To the Oriental philosopher, all nature is to some extent divine, and is valued for its own sake; there is an intimate relation between man and the rest of creation. The Chinese artist who, after years of study and contemplation, paints a shaft of bamboo swaying in the wind *is*, for the instant, that bamboo feeling the wind in its leaves. When he paints a landscape he is literally lost among the mountains; human figures or the works of man are purely incidental.

Though the Old Testament—in the Psalms, in Job, in Isaiah—is full of appreciation and awe of the natural world, still this world was first and foremost a garment of the Lord, significant in relation to a Creator who was above it all ("The heavens declare the glory of God, and the firmament showeth his handiwork"). Man was created in God's image; and the rest of the world was made to be dominated and used by man: "Be fruitful, and multiply, and replenish the earth and *subdue* it: and have dominion over the fish of the sea, and over the fowls of the air, and over every living thing that moveth upon the earth." From here it was only a short step to the philosophy that whatever was not "useful" was somehow vicious, and to the still prevalent idea that the natural world is merely a commodity to be exploited.

Whereas the Chinese had a religious fervor for wild places, to the primitive Western mind they were wastelands inhabited by evil spirits. The fear of God—or the fear of gods—was apparently a potent factor in determining the attitude of our ancestors toward wilderness. Langdon Warner has contrasted this Western attitude with the animism of Japan, where emphasis is "on gratitude to the beneficent forces of nature rather than appeasing the dreadful ones." And in comparing the Eastern and the Western painters' approach to landscape, Benjamin Rowland points out that whereas in Greece a dryad or wood nymph *per-sonified* a grove or a tree, in China and Japan the grove or tree itself was divine. Later on, in the Middle Ages, these Greek gods became demons to plague holy men in the woods, as robbers plagued early travelers. "For more than a thousand years," says Rowland, "wilderness became a kind of symbol of the sinful and unholy. . . . It was only in the seventeenth century, when the demons and the dangers were cleared out from the underbrush, that there began a serious and philosophic speculation about nature and a poetic and artistic interpretation of her moods."

Returning to the Greeks, we find in Homer an abundance of similes from wild nature, though Ruskin claims that "every Homeric landscape, intended to be beautiful, is composed of a fountain, a meadow, and a shady grove. . . . Homer, living in mountainous and rocky countries, dwells delightedly on all the flat bits." It has been said that the Greek ideal was the sort of landscape we associate with a garden rather than with wilderness. The Romans, of course, carried much further this delight in the natural scene, in the land, in agriculture, in country living—in the mountains and by the sea. Yet it would seem that they, like the Greeks, had a greater love for gentle and orderly landscape than for wild areas and craggy peaks. Livy speaks of *"foetidus Alpinum."* Lucretius says that mountains are to be avoided, and Cicero grudgingly remarks that any place where you happen to live eventually becomes pleasing, "even though it be a mountain or a forest." The identification of mountains with wildness is natural, since they were the most obviously inaccessible and unusable parts of the landscape.

During the Middle Ages, the most impressive building sites from the point of view of wild mountain scenery were occupied by the Church: Monte Cassino, Chamonix, Grand Chartreuse, and so on. Beside being cheap—since no one else wanted them—and easily defended, such sites undoubtedly encouraged the contemplative life. There is certainly a connection between the religious temperament and identification with the wild. Many of them already had religious associations. Yet some inner conflict must have existed between instinctive appreciation of the spiritual values of the world around us and the doctrine that this world was only a sort of Ellis Island on the threshold of the Heavenly Kingdom.

With the coming of the Renaissance, with the increasing concern for things of the present world as well as of the next—this attitude began slowly to change. As Havelock Ellis has pointed out, the Renaissance movement toward nature was a revival, in more elaborate and more intense form, of the enjoyment of nature in classical times. It was not primarily an attraction toward wild nature, "but it embraced elements of the love of the wild, and these were notably shown in a new and actively adventurous love of mountains." Dante was apparently a mountain climber. But it is Petrarch who provides the perfect example of the change in point of view, and why it came so hard. In a letter describing an ascent of Mount Ventoux near Avignon, he tells how he was charmed and uplifted by the magnificent views from the summit. Then, unfortunately, "it occurred to me to take out the copy of St. Augustine's *Confessions* that I always kept with me. . . . And I call God to witness that the first words on which I cast my eyes were these: 'Men go to wonder at the heights of mountains, the ocean floods, rivers' long courses, oceans' immensity, the revolutions of the stars—and of themselves they have no care.' . . . I closed the book, angry with myself for not ceasing to admire things of earth, instead of remembering that the human soul is beyond comparison the subject for admiration."

Meanwhile in England, the poets—always the most sensitive indicators of the spirit of the time—had begun to write about nature with that loving intimacy which has always been so much a part of English life and literature. Chaucer's love of nature, with its special celebration of spring, is fresh and immediate rather than literary, though it is confined to the comparatively tame countryside of Surrey and Kent. Shakespeare's plays and sonnets are, of course, full of superb imagery from nature based on a countryman's (not to mention a deer poacher's) intimate acquaintance with the outdoors. It has been remarked how much of the action in the plays is carried out under the open sky.

Alas, in literature as well as in life, "summer's lease hath all too short a date." In the century following Shakespeare's death—the century in which the American colonies were founded—the drift in values and in taste was away from the spontaneous and natural in the direction of the artificial and formal. In literature the neo-classic movement revived and sentimentalized the classic poets' love of ordered landscape. Shakespeare's "darling buds of May" were transformed into wax flowers under glass. Wilderness became distasteful. Nature was tolerated only where it was regimented and housebroken; it was a servant or it was an enemy. Milton could get along very well without "Mountains on whose barren breast/The labouring clouds do often rest." Even Andrew Marvell, who wrote almost ecstatically of gardens, could describe mountains as "ill-designed excrescences that deform the earth and frighten heaven." To see the degeneration in appreciation of nature, read Dryden's "modernization" of Chaucer and Shakespeare or compare Pope's translation of Homer with Chapman's.

To Pope, the moon is the "refulgent lamp of night," shepherds going about their business are "conscious swains" who "bless the useful light." One is reminded of the Mary Petty cartoon in *The New Yorker* of the maid about to draw the curtains: "Is Madam through with the moon?" The sun, according to Marvell, is embarrassed at going to bed in front of the beautiful Maria: "And lest she see him go to bed/In blushing clouds conceales his head." Along with this subordination of the heavenly bodies to the position of liveried retainers, there went a passion for order and regimentation that reaches a climax in Thomas Burnet's *Sacred Theory of the Earth,* in which he expresses regret that the stars in the night sky had not been more artistically arranged: "They lie carelessly scattered as if they had been sown in the heaven like seed, by handfuls, and not by a skillful hand neither. What a beautiful hemisphere they would have made if they had been placed in rank and order; if they had all been disposed into regular figures, and the little ones set with due regard to the greater, and then all finished and made up into one fair piece or great composition according to the rules of art and symmetry."

You can't go much further than that. To be sure, the compulsion to domesticate the universe did allow a few grudging exceptions. Addison, for example, admits that the Alps "fill the mind with an agreeable kind of Horror." But it was his contemporary, the Earl of Shaftesbury, who confessed without apology to a passion for primitive landscape "with all the horrid graces of the wilderness itself,"

as opposed to "the formal mockery of princely gardens."
(A note here on the word "horrid." Obviously it didn't
have precisely the same connotation to Addison and Shaftesbury that it does to us. Originally it meant "bristling,"
"shaggy," "rough." Only later did it come to mean dis-
agreeable or unpleasant. In the eighteenth century it must
have been somewhere betwixt and between.) Far be it from
him, said Shaftesbury, to condemn a joy that is from
Nature.

A generation after Addison and Shaftesbury, James
Thomson shows in his *Seasons* a firsthand knowledge of
nature that is a relief after the classical conventions, though
he is not greatly concerned with wildness as such. Thomas
Gray had an ambivalent attitude toward the "magnificent
rudeness" of the Alps, where "you meet with all the beauties so savage and horrid a place [here we go again!] can
present to you"; though he did think that Alpine scenery
"carries the permission of mountains to be frightful almost
too far."

These were straws in a shifting wind. Quite suddenly,
in terms of history, there arose a whole new attitude toward wilderness during the second half of the eighteenth
century, at about the time that America was becoming a
nation. One can see it occurring almost within a single
generation. For example, in 1754 Oliver Goldsmith is comparing the "dismal landscape" of the Scottish highlands
with the elegance of the well-cultivated plains of Holland,
while the young historian Edward Gibbon makes a tour
of Switzerland without paying any attention whatever to
the scenery. Yet only thirty years later Gibbon himself,
referring to this trip in his autobiography, remarks on how
fashions have been changed meanwhile "by foreign trav-

ellers who seek the sublime beauties of nature." Only a few years after Gibbon's death Wordsworth began to write some of the greatest nature poetry in English literature. What had happened?

One thing that had happened was the publication, in 1760, of Rousseau's *La Nouvelle Héloïse.* Jean Jacques Rousseau is generally given the chief credit for the shift in attitude toward wild nature—which more or less corresponded, in terms of literature and art, to the shift from neo-classicism to romanticism. In contrast to Mme de Staël, who is said to have closed the curtains of her carriage as she passed the Alps (which she described, with some lack of originality, as *"une magnifique horreur"*), Rousseau preached the gospel of nature in ecstatic terms. He himself must have been pretty hard to take. He rhapsodizes and swoons at everything outdoors; sunrise, breezes, flowers, birds, trees, torrents, precipices. He was not a mountaineer; he liked a good road with a parapet to prevent accidents—which in the circumstances was probably just as well. Though this ceaseless rapture becomes rather cloying, and though he had a streak of morbid sentimentality, Rousseau certainly performed an immense service in breaking the old patterns of thought, in bringing about a new sensibility and awareness of the out-of-doors. He had a large part in popularizing the so-called romantic view of nature that reached its finest expression in Wordsworth. As Alfred North Whitehead says, "Nature-poetry of the romantic revival was a protest on behalf of the organic view of nature . . . a protest on behalf of value." The theological view of the Puritans, which is still dominant in Milton, the mechanistic, anthropocentric view of the eighteenth century, is at last replaced—in Wordsworth's

"Prelude" and "Tintern Abbey," in Shelley's "Mont Blanc" —by a sense of identification with the rest of nature; a willingness to value it for its own sake, on its own terms, which is not unlike that of the Chinese. Though the English poets may have had little firsthand knowledge of wilderness as such, they were the spiritual ancestors of today's conservationists who are trying to get across the idea that wild nature, like the artistic creations of man, is important not just for some specific purpose, but for itself.

Meanwhile, what about the Englishmen who had crossed the Atlantic and really knew the wilderness, on a grand and terrifying scale, at first hand? To the early settlers the virgin forest was anything but romantic. It was an enemy to be conquered. And that is natural enough. If you have ever tramped hour after hour through one of our remaining fragments of primeval forest where the ground is a tangle of roots and the sun barely penetrates through the dense green canopy, you will understand what the frontiersman was up against in clearing an open patch for a stand of corn. And in New England, even if he were able to appreciate the grandeur as well as the challenge of his environment, his Puritan training—his suspicion of beauty divorced from utility—would put a damper on any such delights. To Michael Wigglesworth, writing in 1662, everything beyond the cleared area of the settlements was

A waste and howling wilderness,
Where none inhabited
But hellish fiends, and brutish men
That Devils worshipped.

Yet there were exceptions. Jonathan Edwards had a deep appreciation of wild solitudes and rugged natural beauty, which he reconciled with his religion by considering all worldly splendors to be mere shadows of the awful majesty of God. And there is a magnificent passage from Samuel Sewall which suggests that even the Puritans felt in their bones that man's salvation lay in his fellowship with nature, rather than his dominion over it. Judge Sewall, in the very year that he stood before the congregation of the Old South Church to confess his error in condemning the Salem witches, published an esoteric theological tract about the world to come. In the midst of it his mind strayed to the beloved Plum Island of his boyhood: "As long as *Plum Island* shall faithfully keep the commanded Post; Notwithstanding all the hectoring Words, and hard Blows of the proud and boisterous Ocean; As long as any Salmon, or Sturgeon shall swim in the stream of *Merrimack*, or any Perch, or Pickeril, in *Crane Pond;* As long as the Sea-Fowl shall know the Time of their coming, and not neglect seasonably to visit the Places of their Acquaintance; As long as any Cattel shall be fed with the Grass growing in the Medows, which do humbly bow down themselves before *Turkie-Hill;* As long as any Sheep shall walk upon *Old Town Hills,* and shall from thence pleasantly look down upon the *River Parker,* and the fruitful Marshes lying beneath; As long as any free and harmless Doves shall find a White Oak, or other Tree within the Township, to perch, or feed, or build a careless Nest upon; and shall voluntarily present themselves to perform the office of Gleaners after Barley-Harvest; As long as Nature shall not grow Old and dote; but shall constantly remember to give the rows of Indian Corn their education, by Pairs; So long shall Christians be born there; and being first made meet, shall from thence be Translated, to be made partakers of the Inheritance of the Saints in Light."

Written only a generation later, this is a far cry from Wigglesworth. Of course the frontier was rapidly retreating. Before the time of the American Revolution a good deal of the howling wilderness had been subdued with fire and axe; and the hellish fiends, who had proved no match for the saints, were about to be reborn at a safe distance as noble savages. As early as 1756 John Adams was writing complacently in his diary about the wonderful way in which we had subdued the land to our will: "Then the whole continent was one continued dismal wilderness, the haunt of wolves and bears and more savage men. Now the forests are removed, the land covered with fields of corn, orchards bending with fruit, and the magnificent habitations of rational and civilized people."

Yet there was also growing up a scientific interest in American flora and fauna. Benjamin Franklin was interested in nature as he was in everything else. His approach was practical rather than aesthetic. He encouraged conservation, and surely approved a paper read by a member of the Philosophical Society in 1789, which was concerned with more than timber values: "Our stately forests are a natural treasure, deserving the solicitous care of the patriotic philosopher and politician." The French botanist André Michaux, whose diary I quoted in an earlier chapter, had recently made his journey through the southern Appalachians, amid the stateliest forests east of the Rockies. Jefferson of course had more than an amateur knowledge of natural science, combined with a trained eye for the beauties of nature. One of his principal advisers in the field of natural history was William Bartram, whose father, John Bartram, had established our first botanical garden near Philadelphia. William Bartram's account of his travels through the wilderness of our southern states—while the minutemen were fighting at Concord, while Jefferson was drafting the Declaration of Independence—was finally published in 1791. In France it had an immediate impact on Chateaubriand, who had himself made a romantic trip to America in search of the northwest passage that same year. To the English Lake poets it was a source of inspiration. For instance, as John Livingston Lowes demonstrated in that classic study of the literary imagination, *The Road to*

Xanadu, Coleridge was steeped in Bartram when he wrote "Kubla Khan." The "caverns measureless to man" through which Alph, the sacred river, ran, are the limestone rocks of Florida. In fact, Coleridge's Note Book contains a pretty good description of the sort of thing that modern conservationists are fighting to preserve: "—Some wilderness-plot, green and fountainous and unviolated by Man."

From the early nineteenth century onwards the American wilderness had an increasing impact on our culture, both in literature and in art. James Fenimore Cooper found in it the inspiration for his romances. Washington Irving, though still writing in the European tradition, waxed eloquent over the American scene: "her mighty lakes, like oceans of liquid silver; her mountains, with their bright aerial tints; her valleys, teeming with wild fertility . . ." William Cullen Bryant, for all his worship of Wordsworth, preferred American scenery to anything he saw abroad. So with the artists: Thomas Cole and the Hudson River School; George Catlin, the first painter of the American West; Charles Bodmer, who traveled up the Yellowstone in 1833, one year after Catlin, in company with the German naturalist Prince Maximilian; Alfred Miller, whose water colors are our freshest on-the-spot record of the frontier; the great ornithologist Alexander Wilson, a pupil of William Bartram; John James Audubon, whose work has become a part of our cultural tradition. Artists and writers together—Audubon was both—had by mid-century established a new attitude toward wild nature. It is somehow fitting that Cooper's most popular book, *The Last of the Mohicans*, and Audubon's most popular print, "The Wild Turkey" (Plate 1 in the elephant folio), should have been born together in 1826. Both men were

romantics, both preferred wild America to the studied beauties of the European landscape, both resented the senseless waste of our treasures.

The first American wholly committed to the values of wild nature was Henry David Thoreau. He was, I think, even more of a poet and a prophet than a naturalist. He was a prophet crying *for* the wilderness. As early as his Harvard commencement address, he made the point—in violent contrast to the Puritan tradition—that the world is more to be enjoyed than used. For Thoreau, "the most alive is the wildest." He felt that there were enough champions of civilization. He wanted to speak for "absolute freedom and wildness . . . to regard man as an inhabitant, as a part and parcel of Nature." He identified himself with nature as completely, perhaps, as the Oriental philosophers whom he delighted to read. He felt wiser in all respects for knowing that there was a minnow in the brook: "Methinks I have need even of his sympathy, and to be his fellow in a degree." In his journal he tells how he watched from far off the felling of one of the last great pines on Fairhaven Hill. He might be describing the assassination of a king.

Thoreau said that when he went out for a walk with no particular objective in mind, his inner compass always settled between west and south-southwest. The West to him was "but another name for the Wild." Of course he saw the Far West only in his imagination. Its prophet was to be a man in some ways like Thoreau, in others very different.

John Muir also rejected the idea that the world was made especially for man. "Whole kingdoms of creatures enjoyed existence and returned to dust ere man appeared to claim them. After human beings have also played their part in Creation's plan, they too may disappear without any general burning or extraordinary commotion whatever." Yet men "are painfully astonished whenever they find anything, living or dead, in all God's universe, which they cannot eat or render in some way what they call useful to themselves." Muir's comments and Thoreau's are sometimes almost identical: "In Wildness," wrote Thoreau, "is the preservation of the World." "In God's wildness," wrote Muir, "lies the hope of the world." Thoreau had concluded that most of his neighbors lived lives of quiet desperation; Muir considered all people in towns more or less sick: "There is not a perfectly sane man in San Francisco."

Muir, however, was not the philosopher, the mystic, that Thoreau was. He could find God in a water ouzel, but he could never have gone round the world by the Old Marlborough Road. When Muir talks about wilderness he means wilderness on the grand scale, giant redwoods and the High Sierra, not a blueberry patch or a swamp along the Concord River. He was dedicated to an idea; he was also canny and practical. He could get on with people as well as with woodchucks.

It is well that he could. The time had come to back up philosophical speculation with political action. In Europe the virgin wilderness had disappeared little by little, virtually unnoticed. In America, perhaps because of the dramatic speed with which we raped the land, a cry arose at last to save something of what was left. And owing to our political tradition, it was to be saved not in the form of huge private estates or hunting preserves, but as national parks for the enjoyment of all the people.

On June 25, 1864, while General Sherman was preparing to destroy as much of Georgia as possible, President

Lincoln signed a Congressional bill to save from commercial exploitation Yosemite Valley and its giant redwoods. Frederick Law Olmsted, the great proponent of the park idea, administered the area under the aegis of the state of California, until he had to go back east to take over Central Park in New York City. Though it began as a state park, Yosemite set the precedent when Yellowstone National Park was established eight years later. Here was the beginning of the national park system. A new idea had been born. As the zoologist A. Starker Leopold has pointed out, it is the first example in recorded history of sustained effort on the part of any people to preserve native landscape for its own sake—an example which has since been followed throughout the world. Nor is it surprising that this now world-wide movement should have originated in America. Here man's destruction of his environment has been most rapid, most efficient; here, until fairly recently, we had room enough to lay waste, to consume, and to move on. The founding of the park system coincided with the demise of the frontier, with the realization that we could no longer simply live *off* the country, but from now on we must live *with* it.

The growth of our system of national parks and forests is a long and complex story in itself. The three main chapters in the story show a development in our sense of natural values. First the emphasis was on the preservation of geological wonders. Later came the protection—sometimes misguided—of flora and fauna. Last of all has arisen the idea that certain parts of the national forests and parks, as yet untouched, should be preserved for all time as "wilderness areas"—free from lumbering or other exploitation, roadless, accessible only by trail or canoe. This is a relatively new concept—at least in terms of political action—and it is taking hold none too soon. Less than two and a half per cent of our land (exclusive of Alaska) can still be properly described as "wilderness," almost all of it in the West, and under federal ownership or control. Even this remnant is threatened by multiple forms of exploitation: by highways and power dams, by lumber and mining interests, by "recreational" developments and commercial pressures of every kind. The first sustained efforts to preserve wilderness in the national forests by official decree had its formal beginnings in the 1920's, under the leadership of pioneer conservationists and original thinkers such as Aldo Leopold. It received legal status in 1939 after years of effort by Robert Marshall and others. The Chief of the Forest Service was authorized to set aside "wilderness areas" in which there were to be "no roads or other provision for motorized transportation, no commercial timber cutting," no hotels, stores, resorts, no landing of airplanes or use of motorboats except for administrative needs or emergencies. These remain the minimum safeguards for maintaining the integrity of such tracts of land and water within both the parks and the forests.

Today the clearest voices raised in support of wilderness values come not from the ivory tower—still less from the "princely gardens" that bored Shaftesbury—but from men and women who have followed the forest trails, plumbed the canyons, traversed the portages, sought the treasure of the tide pools at the edge of the sea. Led by such organizations as the Sierra Club and the Wilderness Society, they intend to save some of our inheritance for future generations: not temporarily by administrative decree, but permanently by law. They believe that we can well afford to

put a remnant of wild America into a trust fund whose income we may enjoy while the principal remains intact. The securities—as well diversified as those found in any good portfolio—are not subject to market fluctuations: the call of a loon, the splendor of a virgin forest, the blue of lupine on a mountain meadow, the wake of a beaver on a pond at sunset, the smell of a woodland path after rain.

"It is only the scholar," writes Aldo Leopold in *A Sand County Almanac*, "who appreciates that all history consists of successive excursions from a single starting-point, to which man returns again and again to organize yet another search for a durable scale of values. It is only the scholar who understands why the raw wilderness gives definition and meaning to the human enterprise." Science and the humanities, whose divorce is so often deplored, are reunited here. For modern science, while giving us dominion over the earth, has also demonstrated what the poets and artists have intuitively felt all along—man's essential kinship to the rest of nature.

Outfitting for a Trip

ANYONE who has spent much time camping has developed his own list of equipment. A camping list is a very personal thing. One man's luxuries are another man's necessities. There are those who might omit the air mattresses when canoeing or back-packing. We feel they are well worth their weight (the very light, cheap sort, with a bottle of rubber cement to patch them) for warmth and dryness as well as comfort. A canteen of whiskey or rum (151-proof Hudson's Bay rum is the most economical in weight), a couple of paperback books—these to us are essentials. So is a sketchbook, so are binoculars—but not necessarily a camera. It all depends on your tastes.

Some years ago we had our basic list mimeographed. Now we can mark up a fresh sheet whenever we plan a trip, checking the items that apply. Probably no one trip will include all items listed here. The difference between food and equipment for a back-packing trip and a canoe trip is largely a matter of weight. If we are walking, one 40-pound knapsack each is our limit. In a canoe we take three knapsacks and worry less about weight if the portages are short.

This list may be useful for those who have not developed their own:

Appendix A

Tent	Sun Hats	Books
Poles	Paper Napkins	Field Guides
Mattresses	Dish Towel	* Letter Paper
Sleeping Bags	Towels	Notebook and
Pillows	Washcloth	Pencil
Ground Sheet	Toilet Paper	Money
Reflector Oven	Soap	Driver's License
Cooking Kit	Fly Dope	
Grate	Bug Bomb	Fly Rod
* Stove	Shaving Things	Fly Reel
* Gas (for stove)	Mirror	Leaders
* Funnel	Ace Bandage	Flies
* Bucket	Band-Aids	Landing Net
* Newspaper	Adhesive Tape	Bait Rod
* 2-gal. Water Can	Gauze Pads	Reel
Shovel (or	Mercurochrome	Plugs, Spoons
Trowel)	Nail Scissors	Wire Leaders
Axe	Aspirin	
Flashlight	Nail File	Butterfly Net
* Canteen	Sewing Things	* Jars
* Thermos	Safety Pins	
* Chair Backs		Drawing Pads
Jackknife	Binoculars	Pen
String	Compass	Ink
* Light Blanket	Camera	Pencils
* Lunch Knapsack	Maps	Eraser
Raincoats	Pipe, Cleaners,	Fixative
Rain Hats	Tobacco	Glasses
Rubber Boots	Whiskey	

* The starred items will be taken only when automobile camping. You will say "Aha! They forgot the can opener." Not so. It and the scouring cloth for dish-washing live always in the cooking kit, along with the knives, forks, and spoons.

The tent is 5 feet by 7 feet on the ground and 5 feet high. Made of Egyptian cotton, it weighs, together with its aluminum poles and pegs, approximately 5 pounds. We have added mosquito netting, closed with a zipper, at each end.

A Hudson's Bay axe—2-pound head, 26-inch handle—provides the widest cutting edge in proportion to its weight. This is a real axe, capable of serious work, as distinguished from that dangerous and inefficient abomination, the one-handed hatchet. A light grate for cooking is well worth the few extra ounces. A trowel will substitute for a shovel when canoeing or backpacking, to ditch around the tent when there is danger of rain coming in and to provide for the sanitary arrangements. A few yards of stout string have innumerable uses—not the least of which is to haul the food up into a tree beyond the reach of bears. On a canoe trip we put the contents of each knapsack into a light rubberized bag; there may be several inches of water in the bottom of the canoe after a long paddle in a hard rain.

The food list is, of course, even more subject to individual taste than the basic equipment list. The amount to take and how to pack it are the tricky things. The only way to be sure of being fed is to plan a menu for each meal of each day of the trip. Then you can mix them all up, but you *know* you have enough food.

We carry nothing in bottles or jars; glass is heavy as well as breakable. Certain goods will go conveniently into bakingpowder tins, which have good screw tops and weigh practically nothing. Each is labeled with adhesive tape. The eggs are taken in the long cardboard boxes in which they are sold in most chain stores and, with reasonable care, generally travel very well. We have had poor luck with plastic egg boxes (as already mentioned in Chapter 6). We take Pepperidge Farm bread (carrying it on the plane all the way from our home near Boston to northern Minnesota) because it is not easily squashed in a pack, and seems to resist mildew. When planning a trip you should count the actual number of slices in a loaf of bread and decide how many slices you want each day.

There follows a suggested list for two people on an eight-day canoe trip. It is obviously lacking in elegance, or in any challenge to the imaginative camp cook. It is included here to show the kinds of foods that are practical and to suggest the amounts that might be needed. Anyone who is really interested in pursuing the culinary arts over a campfire can find cookbooks devoted to this subject.

Ham 2 1-lb. tins
Corned-Beef Hash 2 tins
Roast Beef 2 tins
Chicken 1 tin
Canned Vegetables 8. We take the small, "individual"-size cans, and find them quite adequate for two.
Bacon 3 16-oz. tins
Eggs 2½ doz.

Prunes 1 lb.
Minute Rice 14 oz.
Mashed Potato 1 pkg.
Powdered Milk 1 small box
Cake Mix 2 pkgs.
Pancake Flour 2 lbs.
Cookies 1 tin box
Pream
Tea Bags

Bread 4 loaves. This provides one piece of toast each for breakfast each day. Some people prefer to take pre-fab toast.

Prepared Cocoa 1 lb. We like this every night after supper. Those who prefer coffee should increase the amount of coffee accordingly.

Rye Krisp
Semi-sweet Chocolate } These are very delicious, nourishing, and tidy when eaten together for lunch.
Raisins

In small baking powder tins:
Jam   Matches
Marmalade Salt

Dehydrated:
Apricots 2 pkgs.
Applesauce 2 pkgs.
Peaches 2 pkgs.
4 or 5 Soups

In large baking powder tins:
Butter (2 lbs.) Sugar
Instant Coffee Peanut Butter
Granulated Maple Sugar (expensive, but makes delicious pancake syrup)

On a canoe trip the food is put in a carton which fits into one of the three large knapsacks. This keeps it from getting too squashed. Fresh fish makes a welcome substitute for canned food, but don't count on it.

APPENDIX B

Conservation Organizations

Most of the wilderness experiences described in this book
were made possible by the existence of conservation organizations, beginning of course with the National Park Service
(Department of the Interior) and the Forest Service (Department of Agriculture) in the Federal Government itself. Anyone who is seriously interested in preserving the outdoors will
soon find himself joining various private organizations on the
national, state, and local levels. He may be unable to keep
track (at least I can't) of how many he belongs to, but he will
soon come to realize that such multiplicity, while naturally
overlapping in many areas, does not represent wasteful duplica-
tion. Each organization has its own emphasis—bird life, wilderness preservation, national park policy, outdoor recreation,
wild-fowl conservation, game management, open land acquisition, or whatever—and each will support the others in matters
of mutual concern. Many conservation problems require joint
action from several directions. To take a very small local example—my home town of Lincoln, Massachusetts, has three
interlocking groups concerned with the preservation of open
space: the Conservation Commission, which acts for the Town
in land purchases; the Planning Board, which has established a

((257

Conservation District to help preserve wetlands; and a private Land Conservation Trust, empowered to accept gifts of land and money on a tax-deductible basis. Each has its special role in accomplishing a common purpose.

Merely to mention the international, national, and state conservation organizations would take far more space than is appropriate here. They are listed, with addresses, officers, and publications in the *Conservation Directory*, a booklet of over one hundred pages published annually by the National Wildlife Federation, 1412 16th Street, N.W., Washington, D.C. Among the many concerned with preserving the American wilderness are the following (all are private, non-profit organizations):

The Sierra Club, Mills Tower, San Francisco 4, California. A pioneer organization of users of the wilderness, founded by John Muir in 1892 "to help people explore, enjoy, and protect parks, wilderness, waters, forests, and wildlife." Located on the West Coast, but concerned on a nation-wide scale with all our scenic resources and the recreation deriving from them. Conducts a variety of wilderness trips. Sponsors a biennial Wilderness Conference and supports conservation legislation. Book publishing program. Magazine: *Sierra Club Bulletin*.

The Wilderness Society, 2144 P Street, N.W., Washington, D.C. Specifically devoted to increasing knowledge and appreciation of wilderness and establishing policies for its protection and use. Active in investigating wilderness problems and mobilizing support for wilderness legislation. Magazine: *The Living Wilderness*.

The Izaak Walton League of America, 1326 Waukegan Road, Glenville, Illinois. Founded in 1922, with original emphasis on sport fishing; now concerned with the preservation and wise use of all our natural resources. Organized in local chapters and state divisions, with national headquarters in Glenville, Illinois.

Appendix B

The National Audubon Society, 1130 Fifth Avenue, New York, New York. Concerned primarily with birds and their habitat, but also with all areas of wildlife conservation. Operates sanctuaries, nature camps, and educational programs including Audubon Junior Clubs and screen tours. Magazine: *Audubon Magazine.*

(There are of course many state Audubon Societies devoted to similar purposes.)

The National Parks Association, 1300 New Hampshire Avenue, N.W., Washington, D.C. To be distinguished from the National Park Service, this is a private organization whose principal interest is the protection of the national parks and monuments. Magazine: *National Parks Magazine.*

The Nature Conservancy, 2039 K Street, N.W., Washington, D.C. Primary purpose is to preserve natural areas, either by taking title to them or by passing title on to some other holding agency. Promotes the study of ecology and education in conservation.

The National Wildlife Federation, 1412 16th Street, N.W., Washington, D.C. Publisher of the well-known National Wildlife Conservation Stamps, this is a large but non-governmental organization concerned with the proper use and management of wildlife and other national resources. Magazine: *National Wildlife.*

In addition to the above, there are two national organizations of a different type: *Trustees for Conservation* and the *Citizens Committee on Natural Resources.* They consist solely of their boards of directors, and their purpose is to carry on legislative activity in behalf of conservation. (Contributions to these two organizations are not tax-deductible.)

On a world-wide scale, the *I.U.C.N.* (International Union for the Conservation of Nature), Morges (Vaud), Switzerland, is a body composed of states and of international and national organizations concerned with "preservation of the natural environment of man and the conservation of the world's natural resources." *The World Wildlife Fund* (U.S. address: 1816 Jefferson Place, N.W., Washington, D.C.), in close cooperation with the I.U.C.N., the International Committee for Bird Preservation, and other agencies, has been established to raise funds to save certain animal and plant species from extinction; its activities extend "over the whole intricate ecological relationship between water, soil, plants, animals and man himself." Joy Adamson's *Elsa Fund* (c/o The World Wildlife Fund) is specifically devoted to saving the animals and wildlife reserves of Kenya.

Such organizations as those listed above provide concrete answers to the frequently asked question: what can the private citizen do to further the cause of conservation? Their publications keep their membership abreast of current issues and pending legislation, and provide the information on which to form an intelligent judgment and make one's voice heard.

A NOTE ON THE TYPE

THE TEXT of this book was set on the Linotype in *Janson,* a recutting made direct from type cast from matrices long thought to have been made by the Dutchman Anton Janson, who was a practicing type founder in Leipzig during the years 1668–87. However, it has been conclusively demonstrated that these types are actually the work of Nicholas Kis (1650–1702), a Hungarian, who most probably learned his trade from the master Dutch type founder Dirk Voskens. The type is an excellent example of the influential and sturdy Dutch types that prevailed in England up to the time William Caslon developed his own incomparable designs from these Dutch faces.